STRATEGY AS LEADERSHIP

STRATEGY AS LEADERSHIP

Facing Adaptive Challenges in Organizations

ROBERTO S. VASSOLO
& NATALIA WEISZ

FOREWORD BY
Ron Heifetz & Marty Linsky

STANFORD BUSINESS BOOKS
An Imprint of Stanford University Press
Stanford, California

STANFORD UNIVERSITY PRESS
Stanford, California

Special discounts for bulk quantities of Stanford Business
Books are available to corporations, professional associations,
and other organizations. For details and discount information,
contact the special sales department of Stanford University
Press. Tel: (650) 725-0820, Fax: (650) 725-3457

Printed in the United States of America on acid-free, archival-quality paper

Library of Congress Cataloging-in-Publication Data
Names: Vassolo, Roberto, author. | Weisz, Natalia, author.
Title: Strategy as leadership : facing adaptive challenges in organizations
/ Roberto S. Vassolo and Natalia Weisz.
Description: Stanford, California : Stanford Business Books, an imprint of
Stanford University Press, 2022. |
Includes bibliographical references and index.
Identifiers: LCCN 2021016218 (print) | LCCN 2021016219 (ebook) |
ISBN 9781503629134 (cloth) | ISBN 9781503629820 (epub)
Subjects: LCSH: Strategic planning. | Leadership. | Organizational change.
Classification: LCC HD30.28 .V388 2022 (print) | LCC HD30.28 (ebook) |
DDC 658.4/012—dc23
LC record available at https://lccn.loc.gov/2021016218
LC ebook record available at https://lccn.loc.gov/2021016219

Cover design: Notch Design
Text design: Kevin Barrett Kane
Typeset in 10/15 Spectral

*In memory of **Arnie C. Cooper**
and in gratitude to **Rodolfo Q. Rivarola**,
two beloved professors whose example continues to light our way.*

CONTENTS

FOREWORD

We are writing this in early 2021. There is optimism in the air and in our hearts. While we know that there will still be difficult days ahead, the availability of multiple vaccines for dealing with COVID-19 gives us reason to believe that the end of the pandemic is within our sights. We have hope that when you are reading this in late 2021 and beyond (because we believe that this book will have value for executive teams and strategy consultancies for decades to come), COVID-19 and robust personal and economic recoveries will be the subject of history and not current realities.

Predictably, we are also beginning to see retrospective examinations of the private and, more significantly, governmental decision-making in early 2020 as the presence and the spread of the virus became more pronounced. There are themes recurring in these narratives that strike a familiar chord with us. First, policy makers, particularly those closest to the world of electoral politics, wanted to believe that the virus was no worse than the annual flu. Second, those who disagreed were often shut out of the key conversations, dismissed as one-note Cassandras. And third, somewhat ironically, the technical people including the scientists, the medical professionals, and the public health experts were those most likely to be advocating for measures that demanded widespread, distributed responsibility and behavioral change. These changes would range from annoying (masks, social distancing, and repeated hand washing) to extremely disruptive (like shutting down most of the economy and schools) to the daily lives of millions of people. They were not saying, "We can solve this. Leave it to us experts," as experts often do. To the contrary, their message from very early on was that, in order to control the pandemic and limit its human devastation and economic impact, people everywhere had to agree to take steps that they were perfectly capable of doing but that would create significant inconveniences and challenging discontinuities in their habits and behaviors.

Not surprisingly, and not coincidentally, some of the most important lessons from the pandemic experience are closely connected to the insights that Natalia Weisz and Roberto Vassolo have captured in these pages you are about to read.

From our experience and observation, the single most common explanation for the failure of leadership comes from trying to treat challenges that are primarily adaptive in nature as if they were technical problems.

Between the two of us, we have been teaching, writing, and consulting about this stumbling block for over sixty years. Our work has taken us from Harvard Kennedy School classrooms to workshops and engagements all over the globe, helping senior authorities across the public, nonprofit, and private sectors address their most difficult strategic and tactical issues.

Nowhere has this difficulty been more present than when corporations try to come to grips with changing circumstances—internal, external, or both. Ron wrote about this as far back as 1997, in his landmark article in *Harvard Business Review* called "The Work of Leadership," which he coauthored with Donald Laurie.

From our earliest days as colleagues and collaborators, we noticed that organizations tended to fall back on strategic planning processes to address the long- or medium-term need for providing direction, a roadmap for the employees, senior managers, and boards. These initiatives typically use the services of outside firms, sometimes big consultancies with an international footprint, sometimes smaller boutiques who hold themselves out as experts in strategic planning. The scope of work might involve interviews and/or off-site retreats. The large firms often bring in a cadre of talented, young people, often newly minted MBAs, who collect qualitative and quantitative data, which are then assembled, refined, and turned into a lengthy report with a raft of recommendations, sometimes developed with the involvement of more senior members of the consultancy, sometimes not. Once the report is delivered and then presented in an agonizingly long and detailed PowerPoint deck, the consultants' work is often done.

What we also noticed was that many of the recommendations were never implemented. Indeed, our impression is that the implementation failure rate of strategy consultancies is upward of 70 percent. Sometimes the whole report is literally put on a shelf, untouched. On many occasions, our small firm, which focused on helping clients tackle their adaptive challenges, was called in afterward to help them figure out why the strategic planning process failed and what they could do about it.

The key insight here is that strategic recommendations are not strategic solutions until they are refined and lived in the hearts, minds, and actions of people.

Natalia and Roberto have traveled a journey similar to ours, from the classroom to consulting and back again, with each realm feeding the other. Natalia is steeped in adaptive leadership, Roberto in strategic management. In their work, they began to see that the two specialties were inextricably linked. With that realization, they went even further than we have done in bringing those worlds together.

Five years ago, in collaboration with other colleagues, they created an executive program with a cohort of several senior teams from different industries, each team bringing to the classroom setting a daunting external or internal organizational challenge. Roberto and Natalia worked with them both as a whole cohort and in small groups, helping them learn how to address their challenges adaptively and pollinating their experiences across organizations so that they could learn from each other as well. The teams worked their own organizational issues, shared their experiences, and benefited from the awareness that they were not alone, that they were not unique in their desire to look for easy solutions to difficult, strategic problems.

Natalia and Roberto observed that the conversation changed when it moved from the purely analytic elements of strategy to putting real names and faces to those who would have to implement, manage, and bear the consequences of the decisions that would flow out of a deep planning process. Some of those names and faces were in the room. In this sense, beginning to treat strategy as adaptive work humanized it, enabling the teams to take into account in the strategy development process itself the small "p" political elements: the needs and fears, hopes and aspirations, and competencies and loyal relationships of those who would need to be involved to realize strategic change.

This book is a product of that experience.

Natalia and Roberto's animating insight is that for strategic planning to work, the process must be understood as adaptive, not technical work. And that means bringing into the planning process all the tools and frameworks that help teams and organizations deal with the conflict, resolution of competing values, and the losses that are part and parcel of doing adaptive work. It means bringing implementation analysis forward so that the strategy development process actively engages those people and segments of an organization for whom solutions will need to be internalized in minds, commitments, and behaviors.

Too often strategic planning processes look for technical responses to long-term questions, as if strategic change is primarily an analytical exercise, postponing a day of reckoning when difficult and sometimes painful decisions have to be owned by many, even if made by a few. Putting off the full implications of tough choices, or not even acknowledging the possibility of their arising, is especially tempting when the firm is doing well at present with no immediate crisis ahead.

Prioritizing is an essential element of any worthwhile strategic planning process. What are the options? What is essential and what is expendable? Of all the values, practices, policies, services, and products that are treasured and have helped achieve the current success, which should be conserved, and which must be left behind because they constrain forward motion?

As a firm clarifies its priorities, inherently it also identifies losses. That's a major reason that treating adaptive challenges as technical problems becomes a ready default. No one gets hurt. Nothing gets left behind. Or at least, one can "sanitize" the losses on a spreadsheet or slide, keeping them at a distance. Too often, the real demands of change confronting firms are left unaddressed or patched over with short-term fixes, like pouring tar into a pothole on a roadway. Whether it is people, functions, or ways of doing business, what had been important and valued that now falls off the priority list represents the threat or the reality of losses to those in the organization for whom what might be left behind matters more than changes they've not internalized. When doing adaptive work, there is often no such thing as a win-win. When anyone makes that claim, you ought to suspect that they are not looking at the real demands of change.

There is, of course, much more in this book. To their insight about the adaptive nature of strategy development, the authors have challenged another default frame of reference in corporate thinking about the life cycles of firms and the ups and downs of global and regional economies.

Yogi Berra is said to have remarked that "it's tough to make predictions, especially about the future." We can call that the Berra Assumption, which provides an easy out for firms that would like to sidestep thinking about the consequences of possible internal or external disruptions when everything is looking fine, at the moment.

Yogi is mostly right, of course. Predictions are dicey. Nevertheless, the authors push back. They use widely accepted research about the ways that firms develop and economies evolve to suggest, as they say, that "unpredictability is overrated." We love that framing. Unpredictability is overrated because believing that the future is unpredictable lets everyone off the hook. It is another comfortable default.

Organizations use the difficulty of anticipating the timing and scope of the almost inevitable stages of growth of their companies and the ebb and flow of the economies in their context as excuses for not planning ahead. To do so would be to anticipate those growing pains and downturns that will be disruptive when they occur. That would force hard budgetary, personnel, and product/services choices today, when there is no action-forcing event. Yet.

"Never let a good crisis go to waste," intoned Winston Churchill sometime in the mid-1940s, although the sentiment did not originate with him. And, yes, crises, like the COVID-19 pandemic in 2020–21 do present opportunities that might not have been possible during "normal" times. Saying that, however, as the pandemic showed, waiting for a crisis before taking action typically means much unnecessary pain and hurt. We get that. Painfully, Marty recalls his first major job as a senior authority when he was the editor of a weekly alternative newspaper in Boston in the mid-1970s. He acknowledges making many mistakes in the role, but in retrospect among the most costly was his inclination to wait for a newly surfacing problem to turn into a crisis before addressing it. He likened it to noticing smoke in a wastebasket but not mentioning it until the room was on fire.

In that spirit, Natalia and Roberto use their classroom and consulting experience to offer their second piece of wisdom.

Given what we know about recurring economic cycles and the typical stages of business development, the size and arrival date of these very likely to occur disruptions is not so easy to ascertain, but their likelihood of happening is almost certain. Thinking this way reminds us of the great work in scenario planning pioneered by Peter Schwartz at the Shell Oil Company and then the Global Business Network. Scenario planning does not try to predict the future, but it stimulates companies to describe a wide set of possible futures and take decisions accordingly today. Having been through some of these sessions ourselves, we are more than aware of how uncomfortable, and important, it is to bring those alternative futures into current planning processes.

If leadership demands sustained effort to foresee and prepare for what's over the horizon, it also demands ongoing improvisational adaptability to newly discovered and changing conditions that emerge as one takes action. Perhaps Dwight Eisenhower said it best. After leading, arguably, the most complex military undertaking in human history, the invasion of allied forces on D-Day, Eisenhower said that the armies under his command could never have gotten onto the beaches of Normandy without planning, but once they hit the beach, they had to toss out the plan. As president of the United States, he said it this way: "In preparing for battle I have always found that plans are useless, but planning is indispensable." We think Eisenhower overstated the case but only to make the point the authors make so well here: planning and adaptability go hand in hand, like structure in jazz. Plan like crazy, but don't get wedded to the plan because the plan is yesterday's best guess.

Through compelling stories and analysis, the authors integrate two large sets of concepts into a whole new conception of strategy development, implementation, and the leadership to make it happen. Their book makes not only an invaluable contribution to every major company engaged in strategic change but also could revolutionize the strategy consulting industry.

RON HEIFETZ
MARTY LINSKY
February 2021

PREFACE

This book marks the end of a journey that began twenty years ago when we were both in a PhD program in strategic management at Purdue University as well as in the opening up of a new conversation that comes with sharing our ideas with a wider audience. After we graduated with our doctorates, our work diverged. Roberto spent time in academia, researching, teaching, and consulting with medium- to large-sized corporations, helping them to understand and address competitive challenges. Meanwhile, Natalia started to focus on developing teams' social capital, subsequently shifting her attention toward the study and practice of leadership. For years, Roberto's focus was on helping companies *formulate* their strategic plans while Natalia helped companies *implement* their strategies across a range of different activities.

As a married couple that works at the same institution in Argentina—the IAE Business School—it has been inevitable that we have influenced each other throughout our careers. What became apparent, as we shared our research, teaching, and consultancy experiences on a daily basis, was that our approaches complemented each other and, together, could be a source of new knowledge and actionable insights. Strategic plans and strategic planning processes, we saw, were not just technical tools but also leadership interventions, allowing for the most fundamental conversations within organizations, particularly at the level of the senior management team.

To explore our ideas further, we worked with other colleagues at IAE Business School to establish an executive program for senior management teams that was launched in 2015. This also prompted an adjustment in our approach to strategic management consultancy, embracing strategic planning as a leadership process. In fact, throughout, our consulting fed our teaching and vice versa. The new program was very well received, and we started to accumulate anecdotes and notes as we developed new tools and frameworks that were designed initially to enrich the senior management team program. We then shared what we had learned with fellow consultants and with participants in other programs at the business school, including the Executive MBA.

In early 2018, we decided to assemble all this material into a book. We circulated a first draft later that year among academic colleagues with an interest in Strategic Management and Adaptive Leadership based in the United States, Europe, and Latin America as well as among writers and consultants based in Europe and Australia. While the feedback was positive and supportive regarding the substance of the book and what it could contribute to the field, we were also advised to make our text less academic, more prescriptive, and more accessible to the general reader.

The book you now hold in your hands (or stare at on a screen), is the product of our attempts to act on this friendly advice and to incorporate contextual material relevant to the unsettled times we have lived through during the coronavirus pandemic. We have sought to integrate different theories and practices in strategy, change, and leadership, among others, providing tools and guidance on how to diagnose drastic competitive changes and then successfully address them. Throughout, we take a holistic view that allows us to specify the mechanisms linking competitive changes with leadership challenges.

Our aim has been to write a book that is equally useful to an academic, a consultant, a business executive, and a general reader. We hope, too, that the frameworks and tools included in the book will help companies to successfully navigate the critical challenges and environmental changes that they will inevitably encounter in the years ahead.

ACKNOWLEDGMENTS

A book is a social process. It is a synthesis of years of study, experiences, conversation, learning, insight, and ideas, which are given light and direction by the many people who participate in their different ways. Here, we wish to thank the people, institutions, and theories that have enlightened, supported, and sustained us along the way while we have researched and written *Strategy as Leadership*.

First, we want to thank Rodolfo Rivarola, dean of IAE Business School, who influenced us both in many ways, not least in his embodiment of the practice of adaptive leadership. We are also grateful to the Business School for providing us with the opportunity and an unbeatable environment to realize this project. At IAE, we are part of a faculty that is eager to make a positive societal impact. We take this very seriously and support each other in helping our students achieve genuine transformation. We have no doubt that much of what we set out here also belongs to our colleagues. We are especially thankful to José Luis Gómez López Egea for having founded the school and accompanied us silently but effectively in this project.

Most of the stories and examples we share in this book come from our work with graduate executive students and consultancy clients. We are deeply grateful to those we have worked with for sharing so openly with us the strategic leadership challenges with which they struggled. For the sake of variety, many of these stories are amalgams of different organizations' experiences. To honor confidentiality, we have altered names and identifying characteristics.

We are indebted to those giants on whose shoulders we gently stand. Ron Heifetz and Marty Linsky not only developed the adaptive leadership framework from which we work, but they also provided us with invaluable support and guidance as the first drafts emerged. Both showed enormous generosity in reading the material, providing us with feedback, and, more importantly, bolstering our confidence in the path we were following.

We are deeply grateful for the intelligent and generous support of our friend Diana Renner. Her experience as an adaptive leadership consultant and as a book writer proved essential in our final framing of the book.

We enormously value the support and recommendations we received from Roy Suddaby, Woody Powell, and Gustavo Herrero. Their trust in us and our work is an example we would like to replicate with other passionate scholars and writers.

We are indebted to Jeff Kehoe who made expert recommendations on an early version of the manuscript, and to Faye Leerink who provided excellent feedback on the final manuscript.

We thank Ignacio Etcheberne, Carlos Remotti-Bretton, Brad McRae, Sally Maitlis, Tom Lawrence, Patricia Friederich, Margarita Gotkun Silver, Hellen Aasgard, Camilo García, Diana Araoz, Adriana Weisz, Luiz Mesquita, Michell Barmazel, Virginia Sarria-Allende, Carolina Dams, and Javier Rodriguez Ruiz for their feedback and encouragement provided at different stages of the writing process.

We are grateful to our research colleagues María Jose Murcia, Javier García Sanchez, Tomás Reyes, Alejandro MacCawley, and Alfonso Cruz as we draw on many projects we have done together. We want to recognize our colleagues Raul Medina Fernandez, Rubén Figueiredo, Alberto Willi, Francisco Diaz Hermelo, Martín Zemborain, Tomás Farchi, Sofía Serrano,

Ernesto García Gonzalez, and Sara Caputo with whom we share many teaching experiences and from whom we always learn.

Richard Martin and Steve Catalano have made invaluable contributions. Richard's editorial assistance has allowed our writing to achieve clarity and elegance. The enthusiasm and guidance of Steve at Stanford University Press was exactly what we needed to help us produce the final draft.

Last but not least, we want to acknowledge the wisdom and care of our family. Our parents, Mercedes and Roberto Vassolo and Silvia and Gustavo Weisz, have no idea how much they have influenced this book. Our eight children, Bautista, Santiago, Nicolas, Fernando, Francisco, Rafael, Clara, and Marcos, inspire us continuously and have been part of this fantastic process every step of the way.

STRATEGY AS LEADERSHIP

INTRODUCTION

STRATEGY AS LEADERSHIP

The task of developing a company's strategic plan is a leadership challenge—strategy as leadership.

Strategy and *leadership* are broad concepts, burdened by many different meanings. For us, strategy is primarily about setting priorities. A company needs to agree on what it is critical to undertake over the coming years in order to survive and succeed. It also needs to identify what is not critical, regardless of the potential benefits of certain products and activities. Leadership, on the other hand, is the practice of mobilizing people to tackle tough challenges and to develop the capacity to adapt and thrive in challenging environments. It is also about diagnosing the essential, distinguishing it from the expendable, and bringing about a real challenge to the status quo.

For years, we have listened to a familiar complaint. When we talk with senior management teams, they tend to bemoan the fact that managers are reluctant to do what has been requested of them. Meanwhile, the CEOs we meet grumble about the other members of their senior team, observing that they are weak at fulfilling their own responsibilities and at pushing others to do so too.

Interestingly, when we talk with employees in these organizations, they complain that for the CEO and the senior management team *everything* is important. They rarely know, therefore, what should take priority or how they should manage their agendas, direct their own effort, or, where relevant, that of their teams.

The failure to set priorities is the commonest way of avoiding organizational change. As change is the object of leadership, not prioritizing is the sneakiest way to avoid the responsibility of exercising real leadership. A vague priority definition guarantees the maintenance of the status quo—something that rarely leads to long-term success or survival.

For years, we discussed this phenomenon with one senior management team after another. Why do companies fail to set priorities? When they do set them, why do they fail to sustain them over time? What has become increasingly clear to us is that the challenge with setting priorities relates not to the benefits that are anticipated but to the hidden losses that are incurred once priorities have been agreed.

The cup-half-full perspective highlights the positive aspects of prioritization; the cup-half-empty perspective sees only the negative aspect of the losses. Whenever an individual or an organization sets priorities, it accepts that certain things will fall by the wayside as they will no longer be the focus of attention in the years to come. Prioritization brings with it a degree of pain, echoing to a certain extent the existentialist philosophy that we are condemned to a life of choices.

A shift from a product-based company to one that delivers customer-oriented services, for example, will inevitably have a negative impact on budgets, personnel, facilities, and equipment for a manufacturing division, its supply chain, and distributors. It will raise questions about pertinent skills and capabilities, affecting recruitment, training, and redeployment of existing staff across the organization. It may also change how, where, and when the company engages with its customers.

One of the most significant challenges is that posed to the senior management team itself. Organizations mirror what happens in the senior management team. If resistance is to be found among its members, then this will be replicated at lower organizational levels too. Setting priorities is a challenge for members of senior management teams who will have to acknowledge and accept their own losses while helping steer the organization toward new objectives.

Strategy entails the setting of priorities. For the senior management team, successfully setting priorities requires not only the identification of a new set of organizational capabilities to develop but also an understanding of the losses the organization will face in pursuit of its new priorities. This notion of managing losses is at the root of our *strategy-as-leadership* argument. Throughout the book, we will draw on both evolutionary economics and adaptive leadership to shed further light on our ideas.[1] We will use evolutionary economics to predict changes in the competitive context, including those generated from macroeconomic shifts, and we will incorporate insights from adaptive leadership to anticipate losses and to address successful organizational changes.

A FOCUS ON THE PREDICTABLE

Unpredictability is overrated. Organizations mostly fail at the navigation of predictable changes. In fact, it is often the case that managers can anticipate when an industry will stop growing at two-digit rates and enter into maturity. However, as we will explore in the following pages, numerous companies exit an industry at the point when it evolves from the development to the maturity stage. Another case that we will address is that of recessions. They are among the inevitable changes in the evolution of countrywide economic activity. However, the year after a recession occurs, bankruptcies multiply.

Because industries and countries evolve in regular patterns, and because companies mostly fail in navigating fairly predictable changes, in this book, we focus on analyzing predictable but drastic environmental changes. Evolutionary economics studies are instrumental as they provide broad context and help to anticipate the environmental changes that an organization will have to address. These changes are a fundamental source of organizational stress as they inevitably request changes in organizational routines, skills, and capabilities.

We take an outside-in approach to organizational change. By screening the environment, we detect the main evolutionary trends. As we plot changes in the environment, we can anticipate what types of new routines an organization will need to develop and what kinds of new skills employees will need to acquire. We can foresee, therefore, both what an organization will need to prioritize and the losses it will need to accept as a result.

It should be noted, though, that while we argue that changes often are predictable, it does not follow that the solutions to these changes come predefined. Instead, companies will need to work hard to find the most appropriate and contextually relevant answers to competitive changes. The sooner they can identify and make sense of changes, the more rapid and effective can be their response to them.

Our aspiration is to help enhance senior management teams' capabilities, enabling them to address environmental changes successfully. We have focused on four different strategic leadership challenges, using case studies to bring them to life. They cover some of the most harmful changes that most of the organizations will face, once or several times along their existence.

We first describe the *developmental challenge*, which applies when an industry shifts from a development stage to one of maturity. This currently applies to the global smartphone industry in which the once steep rate of growth has now plateaued. Senior management teams in this sector are now required to guide their organizations as they adapt to a market that is more restricted than it once was, requiring different capabilities and resources in order to compete effectively.

Our second area of focus is the *creative challenge*, which emerges when an industry faces the radical transformation of its primary value propositions. This is well illustrated by the advent of the electric car and its impact on the auto industry. In many respects, the creative challenge is the inverse of the developmental one, with the industry switching from restriction to abundance. The challenge is to develop a radically new set of organizational capabilities to address this new context.

Third is the *emergency challenge*, which occurs when a nation enters into recession. This is similar to the development challenge in terms of the restriction of demands organizations face, with the consequent increase in competition, although the emergency challenge is more transitory in nature. This is a challenge pertinent to the drastic worldwide economic contraction that has been caused by the COVID-19 pandemic.

Finally, we address the *structural challenge* with particular reference to commodity industries, such as crops, livestock, and pulp. This challenge addresses a commodity-based company's strategic leadership dilemmas when the mid- to long-term commodity price trajectory indicates decline rather than growth—something that has affected several organizations since the 2014 fall in oil prices. The structural challenges place a commodity company in a semipermanent state of lower operating margins.

The unexpected will happen; we know that for certain. However, being prepared for the expected helps to lessen the effect of the unexpected, since unforeseen situations, like the COVID-19 pandemic, exacerbate the impact of the predictable changes. Companies that had anticipated a national contraction, and were ready, therefore, for an emergency challenge, will find themselves better prepared for a worldwide recession such as the one caused by the pandemic. While those companies that anticipated a developmental challenge will have greater opportunities for consolidation, taking advantage of what is likely to occur during and after the coronavirus crisis. In other words, those well prepared for the expected will be better positioned to address the challenges that the unexpected brings.

PREPARING TO NAVIGATE THIS BOOK

In *Strategy as Leadership*, we illustrate the different challenges with reference to diverse examples taken from our own consultancy engagements, business literature, academic case studies, and classroom discussions. These examples illuminate distinct sets of strategic priorities as well as patterns of loss to which organizations have to respond and adapt.

Some of our insights are based on interaction with clients and students where information was supplied in confidence. To honor this, we have anonymized some of the scenarios discussed in this book, using made-up names for both people and organizations as well as removing anything descriptive whereby individuals could be identified.

Readers looking for quick answers do not need to read the book from cover to cover to obtain practical insights. It is not required to follow any sequence to understand each leadership challenge's content, all of which are intended to be self-contained. However, reviewing the challenges in sequential order might facilitate the reader's understanding of the interrelatedness between the different cyclical changes in the competitive environment and the leadership challenges they imply.

Understanding the book does not require prior knowledge of strategy or leadership. We try to explain the basic concepts, and we have included an appendix with more detailed explanations. However, probably, those readers familiar with Ronald Heifetz and Marty Linsky's works in adaptive leadership will obtain additional insights from the book.

Senior management teams that use our outside-in approach to strategic adaptive challenges should address it as a process involving the following key activities: (1) scanning the environment and identifying evolutionary patterns in the competitive context; (2) detecting whether the organization is mimicking the changes in the external environment, seeking signs that a strategic adaptive challenge is underway; (3) interpreting those observations from a conflictual perspective; and (4) designing adaptive interventions based on observations and interpretations to address the strategic adaptive challenge identified. Each of these activities builds on the ones that come before it, and the process overall is iterative, involving repetition of its various steps.

A pervasive and distinguishing feature glues our framework together, as will be revealed by the cases analyzed in the following chapters: management and its formal authority alone are insufficient to diagnose and craft solutions to strategic leadership challenges adequately. At the end of each of the leadership challenges, we provide a framework application summary demonstrating its use for the challenges discussed therein to facilitate comprehension of the subject matter.

Strategy as Leadership is about how senior management teams are challenged to understand the evolution of the competitive context and, at the same time, mobilize their organizations to make sense of these changes. It demonstrates how both are necessary for an adequate organizational response to change and the successful navigation of whatever the future brings. This book is about the art of setting the strategic priorities and helping organizations anticipate and adapt to their losses in order to increase the likelihood of successful strategy implementation.

CHAPTER 1

THE DEVELOPMENTAL CHALLENGE

This chapter is designed to help senior management teams detect if their companies face a developmental challenge. It refers to the leadership dilemmas and business opportunities confronting a senior management team when an industry starts to mature. For example, senior managers of the US automobile industry faced the developmental challenge in the early 1970s, and senior management teams of companies of the global mobile sector faced the same challenges around the years 2015 and 2016.

As our framework relies on an outside-in approach, in order to be able to diagnose the challenges they face, managers first will need to develop specific skills in reading and synthesizing environmental changes. The initial pages of this chapter focus on how to achieve this. We then move on to an assessment of the inner tensions that organizations experience when responding to competitive and environmental pressures. Such pressures are always mirrored internally as contextual changes usually lead to a new set of priorities that themselves result in a particular set of losses.

An ability to read the environment, however, is not a purely intellectual or coldly analytical activity. The exercise of unraveling what is happening in the environment is highly emotional and distorted by noise. Contextual information sometimes is drawn from the media or other specialized sources, but often it enters an organization through the experiences of its employees, shaped by their own subjectivity and emotional filters.

By the same token, CEOs and all their colleagues on a senior management team are emotionally invested in this task of interpreting what is going on in the competitive environment, which renders its accomplishment even more complex. New observations, new information, and prompt consideration of the organizational adaptation are necessary to accommodate change. When we attempt to "read" changes in the competitive environment, it is inevitable that we do so through the lenses of our own organizations, biased consciously or otherwise toward consideration of how we will be affected and what we will need to do. What changes of priority will be necessary? What kinds of losses will be suffered as a result? Will there be financial losses? Will these losses affect competencies? Could they affect trust and loyalty, internally between colleagues or externally between the organization and its customers?

Models about the evolution of the competitive environment are extremely helpful to cope with the emotional restrictions the organization encounters when defining priorities and making sense of the losses different organizational groups will face. In this chapter, we focus on these models, using the story of Howard Head to evaluate the interaction between industry evolution, the changes of priorities that this evolution demands, and the organizational and personal losses that arise as a result.

A CLUMSY SPORTS INNOVATOR

When Howard Head threw himself into a new adventure, founding his own ski-making business in 1950, recreational downhill skiing was enjoyed by a select few, with approximately 10,000 people participating in the sport in the United States. At that time, the only equipment available to skiers were wooden skis. They were difficult to use and, even worse, very expensive.

Head himself had never been a particularly accomplished sportsman nor a rich man. He compensated for a lack of athletic ability with great skills in aeronautical engineering and business as well as with a passion for outdoor activities, of which skiing interested him the most. Head began to experiment with new metal alloys to replace wooden skis.

He drew on his background in aeronautical engineering, where new materials were enabling fundamental industrial advances. After significant testing, Head developed a simple prototype that made use of aluminum, plywood, and honeycomb plastic. They glided across the snow with amazing ease and cost much less to make than traditional wooden skis. From this "small" exercise in curiosity and experimentation, the Head Ski Company was born.

Market acceptance of Head's earliest models was astounding. In a few years, his work had brought about a revolution in winter sports. Skiing became widely popular. By 1960, the number of skiers in the United States had risen to 1.6 million. The skiing revolution became global when Europeans also took up the sport.

As the market grew, the Head Ski Company encountered increased production problems as it sought to achieve a higher volume output. In 1959, the company moved to a new plant. Nevertheless, its customer base grew at a rate that seemed to exceed all of the company's attempts to keep pace. By 1967, the company found itself expanding the plant for a fifth time. Problems worsened when the Head Ski Company introduced a new product to its portfolio: ski poles. The decision seemed reasonable, as, technically and commercially, ski poles are closely related to skis. However, while they were a success, the addition of a new product had a significant impact on operations, creating additional complexity.

The company now had to address both a meteoric rise in demand for skis and the diversification in product lines, with the company's own ski clothing also having been launched in 1966. Although Head's production of this new range made logical sense, as the products all belonged to the winter sports market, production processes in the clothing manufacturing business were considerably different from those required for skis and ski poles. The clothing and equipment also required significantly different marketing strategies and distribution channels.

In the early years, the company maintained a positive balance sheet, at least according to financial market analysts who declared the Head Ski Company's performance a remarkable success. From 1950 to 1965, the company's annual sales rose from 300 to 133,000 skis. To finance the expansion, Head sold his shareholdings in the company from time to time. When the company issued and sold shares in 1965, Head became a millionaire. However, even as the market celebrated the company, Head himself was experiencing a difficult time. The large size of the business and the organizational demands overwhelmed him. He had struggled over the year to establish a large company, but he eventually realized that he did not possess the requisite senior management capabilities to run such an organization.

In 1967, Head appointed Harold J. Seigle as president and chief executive officer of the company. The founder himself stayed on in a more limited capacity as chairman of the board of directors, a role in which he focused on the job of long-term strategic planning. Before joining the Head Ski Company, Seigle was part of the senior management team of a consumer electronics corporation. He brought keen organizational skills to the Head Ski Company, reshaping it according to functional units, implementing operational systems, and establishing specific planning practices. With these changes, business practices at the Head Ski Company began to look more like those of most professional corporations. Meanwhile, as chairman, Head maintained his reputation in the ski market.

Although Head was satisfied with the changes, he found his own role as chairman tedious. So much so in fact that, in 1969, he left the company after selling his last shares. The company that revolutionized winter sports and was known for its gray-colored products (perhaps a reflection of Head's own color blindness) was now in his rearview mirror. Ahead of him lay a mansion in Baltimore and, always, an irrepressible drive to take on new challenges.

Behind his Baltimore home, Head built a tennis court. Once again, his slow progress in developing skills in a sport would lead to revolutionary innovation. In 1971, Head ordered a tennis-ball machine to help him practice his stroke and accelerate his improvement as a tennis player. The device arrived as expected but did not work as well as Head had hoped. As a result, he succumbed to an inventor's curiosity and applied his engineering skills to enhance the machine. Before long, Head had corrected many errors, and the machine now exceeded his expectations.

Head's success prompted him to travel to the manufacturer's headquarters in Princeton, New Jersey. There he requested stock in Prince Manufacturing Inc. in exchange for the new knowledge he had acquired while making his enhancements. This knowledge exchange, together with an investment of US $27,000, earned him a 27 percent share in the company. Prince was a young organization striving to develop a solid footing in the tennis market. Head eventually became the company's chief design executive and chairman of the board of directors.

With Head on the leadership team, Prince changed direction. Traditionally, as had been the case with skiing, tennis was considered an expensive and challenging sport to pursue. Nevertheless, during the 1960s, tennis was increasing in popularity, with more people taking it up as a leisure activity. As a consequence, Prince's ball machine sold well. It did not, however, succeed in helping Head raise the level of his own game. In his mind, his lack of development as a tennis player had little to do with personal ability but could be attributed in large part to the poor quality of available equipment and technology.

As more frequent and intense practice failed to help Head improve his skills, he began to study the rules of tennis and discovered that the racket's total surface figured prominently in them. He innovated again by expanding the width of the head, creating an oversized racket that proved to be very popular, especially among beginners. In 1976, the company obtained a patent for the new product. Along with material-related advancements, Prince's rackets accelerated the boom in tennis's popularity and the equipment industry that supported it. Head became a millionaire all over again. Four years after its release, Prince's oversized racket was used by over 700,000 tennis players in the United States, representing about 13 percent of the national market.

While both Prince and tennis aficionados everywhere benefited enormously from Head's desire to improve his own game, there is no documentary evidence that he was ever successful in the pursuit of that goal.

A FAMILIAR STORY

Howard Head's story is intriguing for any number of reasons, not least, given the subject of this book, the cycle of innovation, problem resolution, losses and defeats, and adaptation in the face of complexity and competition. There is something extremely familiar—almost archetypal—about this pattern. Certainly, it rhymes with our own experiences working with and studying modern organizations. Consciously or not, at both the Head Ski Company and Prince, Head found himself grappling with the challenges of organizational development as the entire industry evolved. Some of the decisions he made resulted in unprecedented success; others were not the best either for himself or the organizations he worked with. We can alter the names of the people involved, the location, the context, yet we can still find many similarities in terms of the developmental challenges that have to be taken on.

Consider another example. In the first decade of the current century, the telecommunications industry faced a critical competitive shift, moving from wired telephony services with high profit margins to wireless and broadband-based services with lower margins. As the wireless industry matured over the next decade, however, once again growth rates drastically decreased and competitive pressures rocketed. Such were the environmental circumstance that informed the developmental challenges addressed by Verizon CEO Lowell McAdam in 2015. Similarly, at Apple, CEO Tim Cook was confronted by a mid-decade developmental challenge as the global smartphone industry—that Apple itself had catalyzed with the 2007 launch of the iPhone—reached a saturation point.[1]

Confident diagnosis is the essential first step in any attempt to remedy a developmental challenge. This requires skill in reading the competitive environment and anticipating how it might evolve. As the Austrian economist Joseph Schumpeter reflected in his 1911 book *The Theory of Economic Development*, such an approach is essential to any understanding of organizational life.[2]

Schumpeter argued that entrepreneurs are titans of business who, through risk-taking and their struggles to make singular dreams a reality, challenge the status quo. They upset the market's natural tendency to standardize by selecting the most efficient processes. In his view, entrepreneurial creations and discoveries shatter the languor of a mature and sleepy market. New value propositions render the market a battlefield as different players fight for their share of it. This process of "creative destruction," as Schumpeter called it, offers an alternative and more effective value proposition to the established order, pushing society toward a state of greater well-being.

Howard Head's entrepreneurial story is one that documents repeated cycles of creative destruction. At least twice in his life, first, when he developed metal skis and, later, when he created the oversized racket, he shattered established orders and pushed society toward new horizons of well-being. He created value for a broad segment of society, making skiing and tennis accessible to many consumers for whom such sports had been out of their reach. However, instead of becoming a source of eternal vigor for the manufacturers, the enormous advantage initially provided by Head's innovations eroded as quickly as competitors could copy them. In fact, as Schumpeter explains, creative destruction unleashes new processes of imitation. Where an innovation creates new value, copycat competitors will soon appear on the scene.

Schumpeter was as interested in competitive imitation as he was in radical innovation. As value becomes widespread via imitation and is distributed throughout a community, the "excess" profits the innovation generates tend to disappear. Eventually, the situation stabilizes, with the innovation now accepted as a "new" normal. Stated in slightly more technical terms, value-adding innovations create extraordinary economic yields. These are gradually eroded as a consequence of the imitation prevalent in competitive markets, eventually reflecting average levels of profitability. After initial remarkable success, the average can seem like a death knell. In recent times, we have witnessed the impact of imitation with the iPhone and the Netflix online streaming service. In all likelihood, we will see something similar happen with Tesla's electric cars, if they prove to be a runaway success.

In nature, biological diffusion is similar to what Schumpeter describes in relation to innovations introduced into competitive business markets. When fish are introduced into an artificial lake, for example, if they find the environment hospitable, they will begin to reproduce. Their energy and increased numbers will thereby disturb the environmental equilibrium previously found in the lake. However, with growth and increased numbers comes a greater consumption of available resources. A rebalancing is necessary between demand and supply. Growth dwindles; diffusion ceases. Of course, there are considerable limitations in such an analogy. All the same, the analogy is helpful in illustrating competitive evolution, some aspects of which are too easily forgotten in the face of a radical innovation.

FINDING THE STRATEGIC PRIORITIES FOR THE DIFFERENT STAGES OF THE COMPETITIVE ENVIRONMENT

The power of understanding the context lies in the fact that it is possible to determine a reasonable set of priorities for each stage of industrial evolution. The *emergent* stage is where all of these dynamics start, typically with a radical innovation regarding how to meet a particular need. Such an innovation usually leads to a significant change in the product. Sometimes, although not always, this results from a significant technological advance. Exploration and experimentation are vital to this emergent stage.

The appearance of the electric car, for example, has arisen as the result of a series of technological advances in motors and batteries. The success and advancement of electronic products, including smartphones and computers, is largely dependent on complementary technological developments in the areas of processors, screens, memory, and batteries. Away from manufacturing and telecommunications, we can see how the cases of both Cirque du Soleil and Starbucks also have entailed radically new value propositions without any significant technological advances.

To be commercially viable, radical product innovation must be accompanied by a new business model. At this juncture, the work of an entrepreneur is to identify a viable model. This means discovering how a business can monetize the value created to achieve a sustainable organization. It requires continuous trial and error and multiple interactions until a workable model is established. During this stage, there are significant rates of product innovation, which should also be accompanied by modifications in the business model.

Once the business model stabilizes, the second evolutionary phase gets underway, known as the *developmental* stage. Companies by now are more secure regarding their value proposition and the sustainability of their business model, and they are predisposed to accelerate their growth. A race begins. Customers yearn for the product, such as when the first iPhone models appeared on the market. Demand for the iPhone changed the cellular phone industry and heightened competition to win the greatest portion of market share possible, with Apple products rivaling those dependent on the RIM (Blackberry), Android, and Microsoft operating systems.

During the developmental stage there is the sense that there is plenty of room for everyone. Customer demand is high and cannot always be met, allowing many different players to cater to customers' needs, thereby diminishing some of the competitive tension. Organizational priorities can embrace new channels, diverse geographical locations, production efficiency, supply chains, and all the supporting processes as the company focuses on growth and seeks to establish a significant market share.

However, with the passage of time, there is a change in the proportion of first-time buyers to repeat buyers, which brings with it greater customer sophistication and discernment. A more saturated market inevitably results in more intense competition and rivalry between different organizations. The industry has now entered the stage of *maturity*. During this stage, growth levels out and many players begin to exit the industry as they feel the squeeze. There is no longer room for everyone, the margins are much tighter, and companies have to offer more in order to entice new customers and retain existing ones. Indeed, it is customer retention and greater efficiency that become the new organizational priorities.

Curiously, it is those companies that entered the market with a niche strategy during the developmental stage that often abandon the industry once it matures, while late entrants occupy market niches successfully. The explanation for this appears to lie in the fact that when an industry grows rapidly, it is difficult to evaluate whether the service of a given niche will be sustainable, but that this is much easier to do once an industry has stabilized.

READING THE COMPETITIVE ENVIRONMENT

A critical aspect of the strategic leadership challenges explored in this book is that they arise not from the errors or missteps of a particular company. They are phenomena of aggregation affecting the entire industry. All the competing organizations within an industry will have to tackle the same developmental challenge as their combined sales reach a saturation point.

There is no one right answer to this challenge, though, and the approach will differ from company to company, as will the chance of success.

In order to detect this challenge, it is necessary to understand aggregate industry trends. This can be straightforward in some industries but more difficult in others. For example, in the smartphone industry, it was relatively easy to anticipate when the market would reach its maturity stage (see figure 1.1).[3]

US economics professor Steven Klepper devoted his career to measuring the cycle of creative destruction, demonstrating the existence of a regular pattern that eventually changed in terms of duration but not process. Klepper divided an industry's lifecycle into three stages. The first corresponds to Schumpeter's period of creative destruction, when companies are looking for an alternative and novel way of satisfying a given need. The development stage is marked by double-digit growth in demand. This growth flattens during the third and final stage of maturity.

In a study involving nearly forty US industries during the twentieth century, Klepper found that, despite ample differences between particular industries, on average an industry's development stage lasted a quarter of a century, as did its maturity stage.[4] His findings illustrated how organizations invested so much effort disseminating innovations, increasing market share,

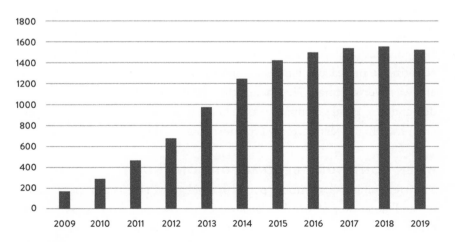

FIGURE 1.1. Global smartphone shipments, 2009–2019. Source: Statista.

and trying to get ahead of their competitors during the development stage. Yet, they should also have been directing their energies toward the capacity building necessary for competition during the equally lengthy period of industry maturity.

In order to forecast effectively for a particular industry, companies need to estimate the speed of growth of aggregate industry sales and the saturation level—that is, the moment at which the product or service reaches most of the unsatisfied demand. The senior management team does not need to do the econometric analysis itself, but the decisions it makes and the plans it puts into action can certainly be informed by the assumptions and results that a company expert or consultant produces.

Having a sense of the cycle durations allows managers to quantify the remaining time the company has to prepare for the next stage. A cycle's duration determines how long a company will spend resolving a particular type of problem and integrating solutions into a set of organizational routines. The solutions themselves will inform and shape organizational values and culture. Analyzing these routines and values gives managers an idea of the losses that different organizational groups will inevitably face when the industry matures.

Howard Head's business life reflects this same dynamic. His company grew rapidly when he overhauled skiing as a winter sport, but in time he suffered the consequences of environmental competition that result from the very industry cycle that he had initiated. Head enjoyed enormous success in creating industries and growing companies, but when it came to adapting to increased change, complexity, and competition, he fell short and was overwhelmed. The change that the new competitive environment demanded of Head's company was so big that he found himself ill-equipped and unwilling to lead it toward the next stage in the industry life cycle.

WHEN CONTINUITY BECOMES DISCONTINUITY

The irreversible passage from a period of rapid growth in sales to one of maturity and the leveling off of sales also involves a burgeoning array of competitive pressures. Initially, these are almost imperceptible because they begin when there is still high demand and low supply. Over time, though, the volume of

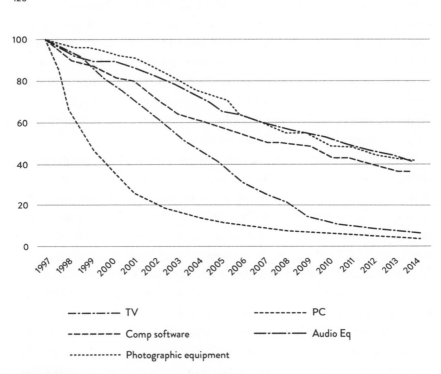

FIGURE 1.2. US prices for electronic products, 1997–2014.

Source: US Bureau of Labor Statistics.

TABLE 1.1. Annual changes in sales and prices during the industry life cycle—average of selected industries.

Period in Years	1 to 5	6 to 10	11 to 15	16 to 20	21 to 25	26 to 30
% Annual Change in Sales	49.8	15.5	8.6	3.4	2.7	1.9
% Annual Change in Prices	-12.6	-8.1	-6.6	-6.0	-3.2	-2.6

Source: Klepper and Graddy, "Evolution of New Industries and the Determinants of Market Structure," 27–44.

customers whose needs are not being met diminishes significantly. At the same time, the existence of an attractive market where demand has not been met continues to draw new competitors. As the industry evolves, and more players become involved in it, consumers become more educated and savvier, learning more about the product and the different alternatives available on the market.

An illustrative way to observe the effect of increased competitive pressures within an industry is to focus on aggregate prices and sales figures. Generally, prices, costs, and total sales serve as gauges for monitoring the competitive dynamics and rivalry in a market.[5]

Aggregate, evolutionary industry phenomena highlight the pressures on an organization's life. With these pressures come the human challenges that have to be navigated to ensure a prosperous future. Systematic drops in unit profit—independent of the relative efficiency of a company—are a strong incentive for improving internal processes, including changing the way individuals work and pushing them to let go of old habits.

Knowing that competitive pressure will increase as an industry ages, can we assess by how much? Is there any certainty regarding what will happen to an industry's members as pressure intensifies?

During an industry's development stage, there is a sustained increase in the number of competitors. When the industry transitions to maturity, there tends to be a dramatic rise in the number of competitors that annually withdraw from the industry. Technically referred to as the "shake out" phase, this phenomenon lasts for several years until the industry attains stability in the maturity stage.

There is, in fact, a remarkable heterogeneity across industries. In some, scarcely any companies disappeared during the "shake out" phase. For example, between 1898 and 1981 in the shampoo industry, only five out of a total of 114 companies ceased to exist, whereas in the automobile tire industry, between 1896 and 1981, 77 percent of its companies were wiped out.[6] Very often, a conspicuous process of consolidation among the strong companies happens. Typically, for each organization, it entails a period of significant stress along with losses and pain for different groups within the organization as they adapt to shifting demands relating to marketing, sales, distribution, and customer requirements for better service or functionality.

The uncertainty that surrounds the "shake out" phase is a hallmark of the developmental challenge that senior management teams have to address as industries transition to maturity. Industry-wide consolidation during this period is informed less by questions of competence than by a changing ratio between supply and demand. Some firms may have overinvested in the expectation of future growth precisely at the time that consumer demand has been satisfied and leveled off.

Two types of changes become apparent: incremental changes and changes that involve a discontinuity. As time goes on, sales grow at an increasingly lower rate. Prices also fall at a lower rate. This is an incremental process that pushes the organization to adopt solutions that address the changing context through continuous improvements, strengthening organizational processes. Nonetheless, incremental change and adaptation eventually result in a moment of discontinuity. This signals an industry's arrival at maturity.

When an industry matures, it is permanently changed as there is an irreversible shift in the level of competitive rivalry within it. This shift will require new solutions to new problems, although firms should not wholly abandon the solutions they developed to address earlier problems. Throughout this time, organizations are bombarded by background noise as their internal structures and personnel face significant challenges on multiple levels. Each of the ensuing changes entails its own kind of leadership problem, despite their intrinsic connection. This is because the way in which an organization approaches the competitive shift will depend on the way it resolves the incremental pressures concerning profits. In the past, during the development stage, the strategic imperative was to ensure fast organizational growth increasing market share, while in the present, during the maturity stage, the strategic imperative is to sustain profits, protecting value share (i.e., the quantity the company sells multiplied by the average price). This change in the central strategic imperative is at the center of the strategic leadership problem.

LIFE AFTER CHANGES IN THE ENVIRONMENTAL CONTEXT

In our consulting work, we have collaborated with several companies dealing with the developmental challenge. Particularly relevant was the story of

Laura García. She was the general manager of Bestclearing Inc., an international consumer products company founded in Latin America. In spite of its global reach, the majority of the company's sales depended on the Latin American market. This was a region that experienced very high growth rates between 2000 and 2010.

Optimal macroeconomic conditions had helped expand the middle class throughout Latin America and were particularly beneficial to Bestclearing. They propelled the company to annual growth rates exceeding 20 percent in its primary markets. Nevertheless, in 2015, the company's outlook turned gloomy: sales and profits, respectively, were projected to reach only 70 percent and 50 percent of the levels recorded the previous year. Brazil was in recession, as were Argentina and Venezuela. In general, the entire region was experiencing reduced growth. In this context, Laura and her team attempted to turn things around, under pressure from the company's shareholders.

Laura asked us to help change the company's strategic direction. There were clear indications that the industry in which the company competed was maturing and that growth rates had stabilized, even when taking into consideration the impact of recession in several countries. In fact, the change in business conditions appeared to be largely structural. The organizational dynamics exemplified the challenges faced when an industry transitions from development to maturity, foremost among which was the finger-pointing and apportioning of blame for organizational troubles between the distinct stakeholder groups.

The first to cast blame were the shareholders, who called into question the value of the company headquarters, asserting that it had grown too big and bureaucratic. At HQ, fingers were pointed at the country managers, who were accused of complacency and unresponsiveness to worsening indicators in their respective markets. HQ voiced concern that the country managers had sought to maintain sales levels by lowering prices and offering better payment terms when HQ believed they should have focused on improving the product portfolio and fomenting the sale of products with the highest margins. The sales department blamed the slow launch of new products, highlighting the product development department's failure to meet deadlines and the logistics department's poor and mistimed deliveries.

Meanwhile, logistics complained of the commercial department's erroneous sales projections that had a knock-on effect on production costs and logistical reprocessing, all of which further complicated operations.

Laura and her team were being tugged in all directions by the organization's distinct stakeholder groups without any clear understanding of what should take priority. The proposed solution that gained the most traction was put forward by the shareholders: undertake an intense restructuring program with the aim of rapidly reducing costs. This would be achieved primarily through adjustments at HQ and the streamlining of operations in each country. Until then, the company followed a matrix organizational design: each product family had a business unit manager and each nation had a country manager. The shareholders' proposal would have required country managers of the larger regions to take on the role of business unit manager too. In addition, the regional business manager would centralize much of the work that, until then, had been performed at the country level.

Laura questioned the shareholder's solution. She believed it would destroy aspects of the organizational structure and capacity that had taken a decade to build. Laura was particularly concerned that the impact on localized structures would be a retrograde step and would diminish the company's effectiveness. While she agreed that the central office had grown too large, she was keen to avoid excessive downsizing, ensuring that adequate levels of autonomy and control were maintained in each country. Laura believed the shareholders were reverting to the company's original model, dependent on highly operational general management but offering little flexibility among organizational units.

A STRATEGIC LEADERSHIP INTERVENTION

Laura wanted us to help diagnose the organization's troubles. In our early meetings with her and the shareholders, the group reached a consensus that the company's problems were more complex than simple cost issues. During our initial conversations, most of the strategic attention was on the main countries' recessions. However, as we pushed them to analyze aggregate sales figures across the industry, it became clear that the company was in the midst of the developmental challenge. This was reflected both by the inner tensions within the company and the external industry data that indicated that it was maturing. Although the situation was complicated further by the regional recession, nevertheless, it was evident that even when this recession was over, growth would be much slower than it had been in the past.

When we shared our observations, there was general agreement that laying off personnel without a value-based rationale for doing so would make the organization worse off in the long term, even if short-term results improved. To develop value-based criteria, we proposed conducting a set of workshops to redefine strategic initiatives that had increased profits as their central imperative. We divided the process into two stages. Initially, we would facilitate workshops with the Latin American corporate team, then we would repeat the exercise with high-level managers from each country.

In effect, this was all part of standard strategic planning. However, the fact that we were thinking about the developmental challenge gave a different nuance to proceedings. As with Howard Head in the ski-manufacturing industry, Laura's company had entered a transition period that would challenge established knowledge and understanding of the field in which the company operated. It would also foment resistance as individuals and groups within the company would react to uncertainty and perceived threats, their internal struggles mirroring in microcosm what was occurring in the industry as a whole.

As consultants, we had been through this process many times before. In the next chapter, we will examine how we helped Laura plan for and implement necessary change in order to successfully navigate the development challenge. Environmental changes invariably necessitate localized changes. Monitoring and diagnosis are essential to detect when those environmental changes occur.

CHAPTER 2

NAVIGATING THE DEVELOPMENTAL CHALLENGE

Strategy as leadership is a combination of science and art. The scientific dimension relates to the capability of identifying evolutionary patterns in context. Our goal is to enhance managerial capabilities for detecting patterns, reading trends, and identifying changes in the organizational environment. The artistic dimension refers to being attuned to the connections between firm environmental changes and internal organizational tensions that alter the senior management team's daily life. We propose that managers take a more abstract and evolutionary perspective when reading the competitive environment. This will enhance their ability to find clues relating to the source of organizational conflict and the reasons for resistance, especially when it is necessary to adapt rapidly to a new context.[1]

To this end, in the previous chapter, we examined how the competitive environment evolves and suggested how to detect and respond to the shifting pressures of industrial change and rivalry. Our aim was to identify the key process, skills, and capabilities an organization will require in order to enjoy continued success in ever-shifting contexts. In the current chapter, we will outline the practical steps that should be taken to mobilize an organization confronted with developmental change, to fine-tune any initial diagnosis, and to modernize management processes.

Our goal is twofold. First, we will propose a sequence that applies to every strategic leadership challenge. Second, we will highlight the elements that are specific to developmental change. There is a situational aspect to organizational planning that makes it unique to a particular company at a particular time. However, the broader contexts within which businesses operate have regular evolutionary patterns. Identifying and understanding the patterns of competitive change will allow senior management teams to more effectively and rapidly determine organizational priorities as well as to pinpoint the sources of resistance to them.

In this chapter, we describe what it means for an organization to identify, understand, and meet a developmental challenge and navigate it successfully. To illuminate the points we wish to make, we will revisit Laura García's story later in the chapter.

A CENTRAL QUESTION: WHAT IS GOING ON?

In confronting strategic leadership problems—just as with any adaptive problem—the first and most distressing question that needs to be answered is: *What is going on?* The process of understanding unexpected and confusing circumstances, working out what is going on, is known as *sensemaking*. Karl Weick, who coined that term, viewed this process of giving meaning to shared experiences as key to collective and coordinated action. The objective is to arrive at a plausible and shared understanding of how to interpret a changing world.

Leading an organization, in large part, requires guiding others while together you make sense of present-day challenges. The effectiveness of the sensemaking process will determine how well organizations respond to their opportunities and challenges, and, by extension, what chances they have to survive, adapt, develop, and grow. A poor sensemaking process can place an organization in a critical competitive situation, pushing it to the brink of extinction. It is unsurprising, therefore, that sensemaking is considered one of the vital leadership activities of our time and for our future.

The following concepts will help senior management teams to improve the quality of their sensemaking process.

THE POWER OF THE HIDDEN P&L

Companies have an explicit accounting statement for summarizing profits and losses (P&L). Changes in the competitive environment immediately affect the P&L statement. However, companies significantly fail to develop and implement strategies to overcome these changes because they tend to overlook what we shall refer to as "the hidden P&L."

The hidden P&L concerns the strategic *priorities* and *losses* that members of an organization have to address. As already stated, strategic priorities relate to what the company needs to do in order to successfully transition to and navigate the maturity stage of industrial evolution. Strategic priorities are much easier to define than to implement since each priority implies a set of losses for different organizational groups or factions. As Ronald Heifetz and Marty Linsky suggest in *Leadership on the Line*, people are not resistant to change itself but to the losses that change involves. It is this latent and unarticulated fear of loss that is often behind organizational inertia and resistance.

Once an organization verifies with some certainty that its industry has transitioned from the development stage to that of maturity, it becomes less complex to make strategic assessments of the competitive landscape. An understanding of the theory of industry life cycles, then, has great value in facilitating both the diagnosis of problems and the development of solutions. It should not be forgotten, however, that whatever similarities exist between the problems encountered by different organizations during industrial transition, their contexts are unique, shaped by environment and internal factors. So, too, are their respective paths to a successful future.

The process of adequately responding to any strategic leadership challenges has three stages: *systemic observation, conflictual interpretation,* and *adaptive intervention.* The objective is to have a clear sense of the new set of strategic priorities the organization needs to implement, detect the set of losses these priorities will imply, and design a list of interventions to mobilize the organization toward its new goals. We conceptually separate the activities and present them in a logical sequence. However, helping an organization adapt to a new environment is more circular than linear. The senior management team will generate hypotheses about what is going on, develop conflicting interpretations, and make interventions that will shed light on their initial conjectures. The learning process will continue with multiple rounds until the organization closes the gap between their capabilities and the new environmental demands. This process often takes years.

SYSTEMIC OBSERVATION

The first task to be undertaken by a company when diagnosing contextual problems and conducting sensemaking is *systemic observation*. Had Laura and Bestclearing Inc. endeavored to evaluate the company systemically, rather than focusing on the garden-variety conflicts experienced in its daily operations, they may have recognized that deeper issues, which stemmed from the environmental context, were hampering results. Systemic observation requires recognition of and discrimination between two distinct planes that affect the organization: the external environmental context and the company's internal organizational dynamics. Failure to do so can inhibit an adequate diagnosis and, therefore, cripple the organization's ability to move in the right direction. However, this can be challenging as events that occur on these two distinct planes can affect and mirror one another.

In Laura's case, early systemic observations would have led people to conclude that the company was entering into a developmental challenge. Aggregate industry sales and profitability data indicated a shift from development to maturity. Given that inner tensions of a company mirror changes in the broader environmental context, several symptoms within the company suggested that the industry's development stage was drawing to a close. This was evidenced by different organizational groups working independently of one another, rather than in a coordinated manner, to attend to the more sophisticated customer needs characteristic of a maturing industry. The internal processes that had served Bestclearing Inc. well in the past now were beginning to crumble, resulting in significant friction between different groups within the organization.

The overriding leadership challenge when transitioning from the development stage is determining what capacities the company needs to cultivate by the time it reaches maturity. Once the industry matures, there will be no return to the high margins and growth experienced during the period of development—at least not until an innovation revolutionizes the industry's dominant business model and everything starts over again.

We can anticipate that the survivors in an industry that has matured and undergone change will be those that invest much greater effort in fine-tuning processes and pay careful attention to planning, costs, consumer demand, and new product launch schedules. While there will be a moderate level of uncertainty regarding which corporate procedures and routines should be updated, it will be far more stressful identifying who in the organization will be required, willing, and able to update their own capabilities. This may well have been what prompted Howard Head to abandon his ski-manufacturing business in 1969.

At the same time, there will always be competitive anxiety. Will we be able to change as rapidly as the context requires? Will we become one of those companies that is just a memory in our chosen market? Knowing that we have to do a better job, paying more attention to profits than sales, does not mean that we have any clear foresight about the long-term organizational implications. With this type of adaptive challenge, uncertainty rests in the subtlest of adjustments. Even if we know what changes are required, it will remain unclear which of our former capacities we can now discard. To claim that the salespeople need to start focusing more on profits than on sales does not mean they should neglect the company's market share or have a precise idea of how the new focus will generate higher profitability.

The exercise of leadership demands that we "get off the dance floor" and "go up to the balcony," moving away, however temporarily, from the minutiae of operational detail in order to gain a broader perspective of what is going on in our organizations and industries. In *The Practice of Adaptive Leadership*, Ronald Heifetz, Alexander Grashow, and Marty Linsky use this metaphor to illustrate how essential it is to gain an understanding of context, multiple points of view, and relational dynamics.[2] The experience of the party enjoyed by those at the center of the dance floor may differ considerably from those at its periphery, while the DJ may have a dramatically contrasting opinion again. The balcony provides an unobstructed, holistic, bird's-eye view of reality. Leadership requires that we keep the big picture in mind even when we zoom in on the detail.

CONFLICTUAL INTERPRETATION

The second task to be undertaken when a company faces a developmental challenge is *conflictual interpretation*. This process entails a significant amount of stress for the individuals involved, just as is the case with any adaptive challenge. It involves working with distinct groups within the organization to arrive at a consensus regarding what is happening to the organization. It is worth noting that this step is still at the diagnostic level. The goal is to help the organization understand the relationship between the new priorities the context demands and the losses that the different groups in the organization will face when addressing these priorities.

Because different groups have a strong tendency to blame others, the risk of getting sidetracked by infighting and personal attacks is exceptionally high. As we witnessed with Bestclearing Inc. in the previous chapter, things can escalate very quickly as one team, department, or function blames another until we end up with a standoff with many people pointing fingers at each other but never assuming responsibility themselves. Matters are complicated further when shareholders demand downsizing and cost-cutting when confronted with a crisis.

Notably, there may be an element of truth in all of these opinions. However, the objective of conflictual interpretation is not to favor one point of view, selecting the "best" or "most correct." Instead, the key to determining effective working solutions is reaching a consensus about the organizational diagnosis. In addition to addressing the various groups' conflicting views of one another, the interactive nature of conflictual interpretation makes sensemaking stressful. Leaders facilitate shared understanding after bringing together and engaging with distinct organizational factions, then have to confirm this understanding with the rest of the organization.

During this process, it is essential to keep at bay the tendency to personalize problems. This is partly achieved by helping all stakeholders understand that the new, irreversible environmental setting necessarily implies losses for every group, even if such losses will affect groups differently, varying in type and magnitude. Most importantly, all participants should understand that the system cannot move effectively toward a solution until the losses that will be suffered have been openly addressed. Conflictual interpretation helps identify the type of loss that will be incurred by a specific group and whether such a loss can be categorized as a direct loss, a loss of competency, or one of loyalty.

Direct losses relate to money, prestige, and career prospects, among other things. Consider the example of an organization that decides to restructure, catering to distinct customer segments and moving away from a product-focused model. This may require the creation of new divisions with customer orientation, managerial responsibilities, and compensation systems. In the short term, at least, managers of these new divisions are likely to enjoy gains, whereas those whose compensation and bonuses were previously linked to the performance of product families will, in all likelihood, suffer losses. Not only will these individuals experience constraint in terms of their remuneration but they also will be subject to a diminishment of power and authority, compelled to adopt a more collaborative mode of working with other customer group managers across the company.

In addition to direct losses, personnel can experience a loss of competence. The fear of having to deal with new organizational demands can trigger significant anxiety. For instance, in terms of the above scenario, a former product manager might question whether they are capable of understanding and serving customers as a segment. The pain associated with this real or perceived loss of competence can equal or even exceed that of direct losses, forcing people to question whether they have a future in an organization that now has new priorities.

A manager at a major bank with strong presence in Latin America, who was much appreciated by his colleagues for his theatrical flair and his candor, said at the end of a five-day, in-house training course, "I'm 50 years old and I don't know whether I can develop the necessary skills for the changes to come." No one wishes to feel incompetent. However, adaptive challenges demand both learning and new competencies. They require endurance through painful periods of uncertainty generated by lack of knowledge and relevant skills. Digital transformation of the bank industry is a big stretch for those who have been in the industry for many years.

Loss of loyalty is another serious consideration. No woman or man is an island. We have loyalties to those who share our values, interests, perspectives, or history. We might serve as a voice for our coworkers or friends. They may expect us to defend certain values and perspectives. Upsetting those expectations can carry a high cost, mainly in terms of identity and a sense of belonging. Returning to our hypothetical example of a sales manager, suppose they have established an informal channel to the logistics manager, going out for drinks on several occasions to talk over their problems. The two have supported each other through various issues that have arisen in the workplace. A restructure and shift in responsibilities could change the dynamic between these two, creating tension, and a sense of betrayal, as one of them is forced to place new demands on the other. Fear of eroding trust inhibits open conversations about the real work to be done. It undermines progress.

When navigating change, it is necessary to grapple simultaneously with the way we work with others and with the values that we have developed or inherited through our shared history. Redefining values can make us feel disloyal to a colleague, boss, or founder who taught us those values or with whom they are shared. Consequently, individual and group conversations that redefine organizational priorities will be marked and influenced by loyalties that must be taken into account and understood.

Direct losses are the easiest to detect. When an organization shifts emphasis from the product to the channel, the product manager has to surrender leadership to the person in charge of the channel—and vice versa. Competency losses are not as obvious, partly because people avoid bringing them out in the open and find it extremely awkward when they do so. In a world in which organizations usually hire, promote, and reward based on competence, it is both risky and difficult to admit to incompetence. Loyalty and trust form an invisible organizational tissue, founded on informal networks and underpinning the manner in which people work together to overcome problems. Their loss can be difficult to detect at first but signals significant disruption to the status quo.

ADAPTIVE INTERVENTIONS

The third task in leading companies to face the developmental challenge is to design effective adaptive interventions that enable organizations to confront complex environmental changes and progress beyond them. The great temptation is to try to solve these new challenges with old recipes and existing routines, dealing with them as though they were something familiar. But a proper response demands the development of new collective capacities. The greatest challenge will be accepting that no one person in the organization has the whole solution to the problem. Every group, every person involved in this process can contribute to a successful transition. Finding the solution is mostly about embarking on a learning journey together and ensuring that it is not ended prematurely by arrival at an already known destination.

The design of adaptive interventions will vary according to the ripeness of the issue across the organization. An issue is ripe when the urgency to deal with it has become generalized across the system, and all the factions are ready to make the adaptive work. If the issue is only ripe in a minority faction, the senior management needs to invest time and effort in ripening the challenge of adjusting the organization's capabilities to the developmental challenge across different stakeholder groups.

Tension and discomfort, within reasonable limits, is a good signal that interventions are being adaptive rather than technical. The lack of enough tension will deter the organization from addressing the adaptive challenges. However, the introduction of too much tension will also paralyze the organization and will make it impossible to make the progress it needs. Throughout this process, it is particularly important to elevate productive tension through the use of objective data whenever possible. During a developmental challenge, ensuring that the organization undertakes an analysis of profits associated with different products and units will raise the heat.

Stated broadly, adaptive intervention during a developmental challenge will entail a change of strategic priority. Instead of seeking to gain a greater market share, the new priority will relate to the increased effort required to maintain the current market position. This will form the basis of strategic initiatives, regardless of the particular characteristics of each business at a given time. In general, strategic priorities will shift more toward maintaining profits. As a result, we have a frame of reference for understanding the flip side of the new priorities, that is, to identify the types of losses implicit in this particular strategic challenge.

Once the organization has come to a consensus regarding the nature of the problem and has defined its new priorities, the next task is to develop an accurate map of losses that the organization and the different groups within it will experience as a result of its response. In the case of a sales department, for example, no one would directly object to better practices for estimating demand, especially when this can translate directly into improved income. The problem for the sales department lies in the privileges and advantages it will have to leave behind when it changes the way it operates. For a sales department accustomed to performance evaluation based on volume sales, a shift toward a profit-centered mindset will require working in coordination with production and other departments. This, in turn, leads to losses for the department's personnel, including direct losses (initially, it will be more difficult to earn a bonus) and losses of competency (it may be necessary to adopt routines and procedures from the other departments, including those relating to performance assessment). Failure to integrate and work collaboratively with other departments will result in stagnation. Survival in the new environmental setting will be dependent on all areas of the organization learning and adapting continuously.

During an adaptive intervention, those that exercise strategic leadership need to establish a holding environment where colleagues can begin to address the developmental challenge. Without a holding environment, carefully constructed to support each of the groups while they deal with the stress of acknowledging and assimilating losses, any action taken in response to the developmental challenge is likely to fail.

The pressure to go back in time to so-called tried-and-tested solutions is tremendous, even to a point where reliance on such solutions seems unreasonable to many participants. Rather than admitting that a wrong decision was made, defenders of the status quo will always find it easier to adopt a familiar solution—and blame the results on external circumstances when the negative effects come in. Finding a strategic leadership solution is a perilous path.

Although many companies successfully navigate the developmental challenge, the journey is painful. Setting out on it requires that leadership be firmly grounded in its purpose. Executives may often find themselves wondering, "Why am I taking the hard road?" or "Why am I putting my career in jeopardy?" Some of the answers to these questions may be rooted in personal interests, but others will transcend the merely personal. Executives who successfully guide their organization through the developmental challenge will themselves grow through the experience, becoming more accomplished in what they do. They contribute to the corporate well-being, helping nurture long-lasting companies, capable of learning.

LEADERSHIP'S ROLE IN THE PROCESS

As the general manager of an international consumer products company in an industry that was now maturing, Laura García was under enormous pressure from within her organization to find and mandate a concrete solution to their own developmental challenge. In the words of one of the country managers, "Just tell me what you want me to do, and I'll adjust the structure accordingly."

While such top-down solutions may have been cognitively easier for many in the organization to accept, the problem was that there was no way for a senior management team located in the company headquarters 5,000 kilometers away to have an in-depth understanding of why sales were slipping in that country. How, then, could Laura know the solution? Centralized, vertically adopted solutions are usually unsuitable when tackling complex strategic challenges. The exercise of leadership requires that we nurture an environment within which different groups can openly interact and constructively challenge the collective understanding of the situation and propose a stretching solution to the problem. The delegation of responsibility to a cross-functional, multidisciplinary team to review important data points, such as the organization's pricing process and relative product value, is one means of generating recommendations founded on consensus and informed by a broad assessment of risk. Such recommendations are far more likely to be implemented effectively across the organization than anything mandated by HQ.

An important question to think about when contemplating management's role is, given that both science and experience reveal that every industry based on a differentiated product will mature after completing its development stage, why are appropriate measures not taken in advance? Our experience tells us that this is because it is easy to accept that growth will eventually slow, but it is far more difficult to determine when this will occur. In general, people tend to overestimate the boom period. Too often, even those with good foresight fail to go beyond abstract reactive planning and to intervene where necessary in order to help the organization understand when it is being affected by environmental changes. It is extremely difficult, without systemic observation and conflictual interpretation, to comprehend or anticipate the interactions that take place when there are changes in the external context within which an organization operates.

In addition to this predictive challenge, management's development of adequate plans of action in advance of an industry's transition to maturity is limited by its classic tendency to return to the familiar, borrowing from yesterday's playbook and organizational solutions that were successful in wholly different contexts. Although these tried-and-tested solutions may lower stress levels within the organization, they only sidestep the task at hand, which is concerned with adapting to a new competitive field.

Those with leadership responsibilities must never lose sight of the fact that even when there is only moderate uncertainty about the requisite capacities for navigating developmental challenges, the organization is still dealing with adaptive change. It follows, therefore, that there is no single "correct" response. As part of our focus on strategic leadership, we help resolve these challenges by providing a framework for diagnosing the competitive landscape. In no way, however, do we seek to determine the best solution for a particular organization. Doing so would mean giving in to the temptation to provide a technical response to an adaptive problem.

Finally, it is worth noting that the activities, behaviors, and attitudes visible at the top of organizations tend to cascade down, informing and shaping what happens at all levels. Employees invariably will mirror their bosses. It is important, therefore, that the senior management team leads the change process, retaining credibility when they have to make demands on their subordinates. The questions that those with authority need to answer will be, "In what ways should *we* change?" and "What losses must *we* acknowledge?"

AN EYE ON THE OWNERS

Exercising strategic leadership is risky. If Laura's focus had been on job security and short-termism, the safest move for her would have been to pursue an accelerated downsizing program with the aim of allaying shareholder concerns. While this would not have been in the best interests of the organization, it would have protected Laura's back. Indeed, most managers would have been of the opinion that it was futile to resist the owners' proposal.

Having embarked on the more difficult course of action, seeking a solution that would allow the organization to address its developmental challenge, Laura also took into consideration losses that can be significant and are often overlooked: those of shareholders. During developmental challenges, shareholders will find that things they previously had taken for granted are now at risk. Processes such as the distribution of dividends or the provision of financing are suddenly under question and are more difficult to justify. It was critical that Laura kept in mind all the risks and scanned constantly for signs of discontent among board members and owners, involving them in the sensemaking process.

Constant scanning implied the establishment of complementary mechanisms. One fundamental was creating a formal round table to evaluate the impact of the strategic planning process's advancements on the shareholders. Another tool was the request for active owners' involvement in the process. Even though the owners explicitly requested lower participation, the procedure established formal milestones to assess the new priorities' effect on them.

The owners attended the Latin American corporate team workshops as active participants. They also took on a secondary, listening role in an exercise that involved high-level managers from each country. The outcome was a standard strategic plan, outlining initiatives for the major countries as well as for the entire region.

Corporate-level and country managers attended the final workshop. Plans were laid out in detail, and the aggregate estimated effect on profits was measured. The plan was approved by each of the family members who were present. Nevertheless, despite their involvement, Laura still found that she had to resist tremendous pressures from the owning family to reduce costs and adopt a centralized decision-making agenda. The underlying rationale behind such demands was an unconscious belief among the family that the company was better managed when they were its chief authorities. They had had enjoyed success, in terms of profits and growth, over the fifteen-year period since they had professionalized the company. However, the first signs that such a level of performance could no longer be maintained, owing to a shift in the environmental context, made them question the ability of those professionals to whom they had entrusted the day-to-day running of the company.

Two months after the process finished, the owners ask for an extraordinary meeting with Laura during which they forcefully requested a significant change in structure and personnel. This signaled a partial reversion to old practices and was a bitter pill for Laura to swallow.

BRIEF GUIDE
to Spotting and Responding to Developmental Challenge

SCAN THE EXTERNAL ENVIRONMENT

Figure Out What Is Happening in the Industry

When you scan the environment, you need to think at the level of your industry, not at that of your company. The most critical information to obtain relates to aggregate sales across your industry. If you are a multiunit business, consider the aggregate industrial sales of the business unit you are analyzing. It is straightforward to acquire this information if your company usually purchases industry reports. In this case, you only need to examine industry sales during the last three to five years and try to detect if there is a clear trend of moving from two-digit growth toward much lower rates.

In several industries and countries, obtaining this information might be almost impossible. In that case, try to analyze industry evolution from your own sales and ask your team about the sales of a strategic group of competitors. From this information, you can infer aggregate industry growth, adjusting the numbers from your company growth.

If the result of this screening is that your team realizes that the industry might be decreasing the speed of growth, you might be on the verge of entering a developmental challenge.

Reinforce the Sense of Urgency by Analyzing the Evolution of Value Share
You not only want to understand if the industry is facing the developmental challenge, you also want to assess if you are reacting in a timely manner. This is where objective data about the evolution of value share can be beneficial.

The value share indicates the amount of value in the market the company retains. That is, the quantity the company sells multiplied by the average price. When companies face the developmental change, the first impulse usually is to decrease prices. You need to ensure that you do not overreact in an effort to sustain sales. As the value share decrease, this might indicate that the organization has overacted, placing the company in a weaker strategic position. It highlights the need to change organizational routines systemically.

Understand the Relevant Competencies for Survival within the New Environment
From the previous numerical analysis, you need to move to a qualitative understanding of what is going on in the business. Try to identify with your team the most significant changes at the customer level. Do they require us to invest significantly more time and effort to obtain the same sales results as in the past? Have the customers become product experts? Is it more difficult to leverage the brand, obtaining higher prices than the competition?

SCAN THE INTERNAL ENVIRONMENT—MAKE INTERPRETATIONS—MOBILIZE
Observe the Inner Tensions and Reactions among Different Functional Groups
You are trying to detect whether your organization is mimicking the changes in the external environment, seeking signs that a developmental challenge is underway. Remember that the environmental change will signal the need to move from a strategic imperative that focuses on growth in market share to one that emphasizes profitability—that is, improvement in total margins.

Achieving this shift requires that the different factions within the organization resist the temptation to behave as if they were in a zero-sum game.

The sales department is the window through which changes in the environment are first identified. Are the commercial managers insisting on more customization of products? Are they complaining that products are too expensive? Is the sales team still thinking in terms of volume rather than profits?

If you are in a manufacturing company, is your production department complaining that commercial managers and salespeople are offering a level of customization that will increase costs to an unreasonable level? If you are a service company, are service providers requesting more recruits to meet customer needs? Do you feel that these different demands put your company in a zero-sum situation without a clear-cut solution?

When you are in senior leadership position in an organization facing a developmental challenge you will be the recipient of the frustration of different stakeholders requesting that you and your team take a stand on conflicts and bring about the solutions.

Make Interpretations

You need to avoid rushing to apportion blame. Above all, avoid personalizing organizational disputes. Keep in mind that the default interpretations people use to explain problematic realities conveniently serve to shield them from the need to change and confront losses. Therefore, people gravitate toward interpretations that are technical rather that adaptive, benign instead of conflictual, and individual rather than systemic. Your job is to steer people away from unproductive interpretations that lay blame on others or promote work avoidance, and to bring them closer to the adaptive, conflictual, and systemic interpretation of the problem.

As people begin to grasp these interpretations, they will legitimize the need to learn new ways, begin to identify the losses that they will have to take in order to make progress, and shift their mindset from work avoidance to conflict resolution. Most important, you can help them think politically, map the issue's stakeholders, and determine what is at risk for each stakeholder group.

Questions are the best way to identify the expected losses for different stakeholder groups. What does a focus on profits rather than volume mean for a salesperson? What does this group fear losing (status, resources, a positive self-image) if things should change? Who feels less competent in the face of the developmental challenge? Where are the strong interpersonal loyalties that could inhibit the change process? Other than functional areas or departments, are there other groups with strong allegiances of which you need to be aware?

How do you answer these questions? The best way is to gather information directly from the stakeholders themselves.

Start Mobilizing the System in Order to Address the Developmental Challenge
You have hypothesized that the company is facing a developmental challenge. You want to test this theory and to include the rest of the company in fine-tuning your diagnosis. For that, you need to start elevating tension levels by using objective data whenever possible. For example, discuss profit in meetings where employees mainly refer to volume. Sustain this habit, as the different organizational groups still will be inclined to focus on volume sales and production, not on profits and efficiency.

A strategic meeting is highly recommended, especially to help everyone understand that you are making an adaptive leadership intervention. Colleagues should be encouraged to assess the strategic environment from a multidisciplinary perspective, with all observations and insights shared between different departments. Ensure that everyone understands that new priorities will emerge from the current competitive environment.

Focus on these new strategic priorities. You need your employees to understand what is changing in the industry and customer needs. The goal is to help the people in the organization look outside, focus on the competitive environment, and develop organizational routines and personal skills that can help them adapt to the changes.

One way to facilitate productive dialogue is to adjust some systems, such as compensation schemes, to make the economic losses bearable for appropriate personnel and departments.

Only after detecting strategic priorities that emerge from the environmental change can you start to empathize with the specific capacity losses that different groups will need to address. Show the attractive aspects of the achievable future, such as clarity about the direction in which the company and industry are headed. Keep in mind that navigating the developmental challenge—as with any leadership challenge—is about setting priorities and managing the inherent losses that result from the process.

CHAPTER 3

PREPARING FOR THE DEVELOPMENTAL CHALLENGE

In this book, we have opted to explore context-related transitions as they represent the moment in which companies face the highest survival pressures. However, transitions are events that happen after years of "business as usual." During the years of relative stability, organizations develop routines with a higher impact on profits. It is important, though, that we remember that the organizational stress that companies suffer in relation to every transition is the result of what they have done previously.

The media invariably highlights the managers that excel in the anticipation of challenges, their names overshadowing the much larger number who are unsuccessful in doing so. During the latter decades of the twentieth century, Bill Gates was at the top of this list, just as John D. Rockefeller led the way in the nineteenth century. Today, it is Elon Musk who is striving to join this select group. What each example illustrates is the need to develop organizational capacity in order to ensure a future for the company.

Managers' observations of the business environment tend to be myopic and biased toward the present. Short-term economic results usually cloud future threats. The higher the firms' current profits, the less likely they are to adequately assess what the future may hold. Myopic behavior is not always the result of an exaggerated emphasis on economic returns. Strategic foresight demands exceptional managerial abilities, and even successful businesspeople often fail in anticipating future competitive pressures. Overall, senior management teams fail to instigate change before it is too late, either because they have not read the signs properly or have been unwilling to endure the pain that change entails, or a combination of the two.

This chapter focuses on the good years, during which there is apparently healthy growth in sales and profits and no suggestion of storms gathering on the horizon. We do not wish to suggest that the good years should not be enjoyed. Rather, we intend to highlight that senior management teams have to ensure that their companies prepare for the inevitable strategic challenges that, sooner or later, they will have to navigate.

THE STRUGGLE TO DOMINATE THE PERSONAL COMPUTER INDUSTRY

The long-term struggle to dominate the personal computer industry has been illuminated by an intriguing race between Microsoft and Apple in the late 1970s and early 1980s. We have already encountered Gates, the one-time figurehead of Microsoft, as one of the high achievers of the last century. But it is rare to find people who know nothing about the life of the high-profile tech icon Steve Jobs, who cofounded Apple with Steve Wozniak and Ronald Wayne. Under Jobs's leadership, Apple's innovations have marked the everyday lives of people across the world in recent years, continuing to do so today several years after his death. Millions of people aspire to obtain Apple products. Moreover, many competitors chase Apple as their pacesetter, basing their designs and services on Apple's.

Apple shook the nascent personal computer industry with the 1977 launch of the Apple II, the first of their products to be sold to the public. In 1980, Apple was the biggest seller of personal computers worldwide with a market share of nearly 3 percent in the United States. The company offered by far the best product experience to customers new to personal computing devices. At the time, the majority of the general population knew little about these products. User-friendliness and attractive aesthetics imbued Apple computers with an enormous growth potential. The entire industry seemed bound to capitulate at Apple's feet.

The story played out quite differently, though. After a brilliant kickoff, and having achieved market dominance, Apple's market share began to plummet in an apparently irreversible trend. It was incapable of overcoming the competition of lower-cost IBM computers. Years went by, and Steve Jobs seemed unable to find a solution to strengthen Apple's competitive market position, investing much of his energy in the development of the first Apple Macintosh, which eventually was launched in 1984. The situation becomes more disquieting when we consider product quality. In several respects, Apple's computers were highly superior to those of its competitors, yet it still failed to dominate the market and implement its value proposition on a massive scale.

The initial failure of the Mac, prior to Jobs's departure from the company in 1985, masks a truth that seems abstract at first glance but that must be understood to define strategic priorities during the startup phase of an industry. During this phase, there are additional competitive dynamics that limit companies' strategic freedom. These dynamics are so strong that trying to bypass them may cost the organization its survival, even when a superior product is involved.

Microsoft focused on the essential functionality that people desired in the early days of personal computing: the possibility to share files. Instead of offering a superior software or hardware experience, Microsoft concentrated on the operating system that was the primary enabler for sharing applications. Together with IBM, it launched the MS-DOS operating system in 1981, subsequently introducing the graphical user interface Microsoft Windows in 1985. In 1990, the company finished the system lock-in when it bundled its productivity applications Word, Excel, and PowerPoint together as Microsoft Office. When Office was launched, Microsoft's worldwide market share in the operating system industry was close to 85 percent. Apple, instead, was fighting to sustain an increasingly irrelevant niche position in the industry.

In 1997, Apple was on the verge of bankruptcy. Steve Jobs returned that year, promoting Jony Ive to the post of senior vice president of industrial design and initiating an innovation process that is practically unrivaled in the annals of business history. In 1998, Tim Cook was recruited as senior vice president for worldwide operations. He brought Apple fundamental skills for corporate organization and planning. Since that time, Apple has become a leader in technology and product innovation, a darling of Wall Street, and a Silicon Valley model that others seek to emulate. For several consecutive years, in fact, *Fortune* magazine named Apple as the most admired company in the world, building its reputation on the back of a new range of products and services that included the iPod, iPhone, and iPad.

It seems paradoxical, therefore, that despite Apple's extensive success with different business lines, it never regained its leadership of the personal computer market. The Mac—Apple's emblematic computer that revolution-ized the industry and households—is today an excellent platform to lever-age other Apple products. Yet the company's global share of the personal computer market barely reached 11 percent in 2018.[1] So, what went wrong? How is it possible that Apple's leadership—which took various products to absolute dominance in their distinct product categories—could not return Apple personal computers to their prior dominance?

HOW MANY COMPETITORS WILL SURVIVE IN MY INDUSTRY?

An industry could be defined as a relatively uniform way of doing things in order to deliver a given product or service that meets the needs of a relatively homogenous consumer group. Therefore, an industry may be understood as a context in which viable alternative business models are developed.

Although industries do not preestablish the manner in which firms in the industry are going to compete, the industry does establish rules for the game that define how firms cannot compete. Creating a business strategy requires defining the competitive elements and mechanics on which the company's differentiation will be built. Industries demarcate the mecha-nisms that a company may build.

Industries have unique characteristics that a firm's management team must understand before outlining its strategy. Otherwise, the firm is likely to be "pushed" out of the market. This is a basic ground rule that increases in importance when aggregate demand for a firm's products grows to two digits, as high growth rates often conceal errors in the company's efforts to construct its competitive position. Mistakes will be uncovered when the industry's growth breaks and causes competitive rivalry to peak, signaling the start of the developmental challenge. Unfortunately, at that moment, it is likely to be too late to build the necessary defense mechanisms.

The late 1970s were witness to phenomenal processes of social collaboration. Certain conditions made it the opportune moment for this to happen, including the introduction of and access to personal computers, the ability to share information between computers made by different manufacturers, and the chance for people to develop their own programs and share them with relative freedom and ease. The personal computer industry required the formation of a community that worked under the same set of rules. The work of distinct actors was deeply interwoven, thereby generating what is referred to in economics as "network externalities," the interdependency of a community necessary to its existence. Such a community required rules and shared standards.

In the personal computer industry, the standard would become an operating system because it was the key to enabling the integration of all variables and information. The organization that managed to establish the standard would have a formidable defense against competitors' attacks: the protection of the community. To Apple's misfortune, many of Jobs's decisions in the late 1970s and early 1980s regarding computer design cut strongly against the forging of a community. The community's development was delayed and almost stunted by Apple's decision to build computers composed of a closed system in which the operating software was intrinsically linked to hardware that only Apple offered.

While Apple incurred higher costs to achieve product quality, its competitors focused on a single link of the value chain: the ability to work as a community with respect to information and software development. So compelling was the users' need to share that they were willing to move to a markedly inferior product if they had this capability.

We can observe a similar competitive context relating to e-commerce and streaming services today. Amazon and Netflix, for example, are two companies dealing with a similar situation to that experienced by Apple and Microsoft in the late 1970s. They are in the middle of a race for market share, and they face some degree of uncertainty regarding the final competitive space when the industry matures. There is a degree of guesswork involved, anticipating what the industry will look like in the future, what room there will be for rival organizations, and what competitive isolating mechanisms will be in place.

Governments and economists were the first to focus on these mechanisms. The reason for this was practical: some industries had fewer competitors than others, and the lesser the number of players in an industry, the further the average price of its products was from optimum prices for consumers. Price increases that came along with industry concentration negatively affected the general well-being and product innovation levels. In a nutshell, society seemed worse off. As a result, economic science delved into understanding what leads to the consolidation of competitors in an industry.

These observations trace back to the nineteenth century and are exemplified by the notorious case of the Standard Oil Company. At that time, a significant number of oil companies were created in the United States. However, by the end of that century, participation in the oil business was reduced to a single competitor: the Standard Oil Company, led by John D. Rockefeller. This consolidation was the result of a deft and arduous scheme of mergers, acquisitions, and competitive conquests. Why was Rockefeller able to secure a monopoly? Much has been written on this topic, especially descriptions of Rockefeller's business practices and his aggressive ambitions. Notwithstanding, the business conduct that consolidated Standard Oil's monopoly was only possible because there existed objective data regarding the industry's business model indicating that the industry was ripe for strong consolidation. From a standpoint of economies of scale and distribution, the Standard Oil Company built formidable mechanisms of competitive isolation.

Countless supporting studies revealed that such opportunities are available only at certain times and that those who fail to seize them can be left out of the game or compelled to adopt a niche position in the future. These studies also found that identifying these competitive spaces requires comprehensive observation of the industry, determining its minimum size and optimal growth rate. In the operating systems business, competitive exclusion was possible at the consumer level, as consumers required a standard to share information. Because of the large number of competitors, this meant that attaining the greatest and fastest consumer adoption was the key to success. Bill Gates understood these processes with an admirable mastery. His strategic move was to accelerate the introduction of Windows into the market, giving the product away and allowing for the multiplication of unauthorized copies.

Each industry has its own competitive isolating forces, and a fundamental managerial skill is to anticipate them. These factors must be identified in a timely fashion, when the industry is still in a developmental stage. Only by early identification can a company adopt a sustainable position and build the necessary market share, growing at the minimum necessary rate to ensure survival conditions on the industry's entrance into the maturity phase.

DOUBTING THE FUTURE

We have encountered senior managers trying to anticipate the competitive isolating forces on numerous occasions in our consulting activity. Sofía Nevares, for example, owned and managed Home Healthcare Services, a company dedicated to home care. This had been founded by her parents in Argentina, and they were still involved in the business decision-making process. Many of the national competitors were of similar size. Sofía knew her company was among the biggest in the sector, which was composed of about twenty organizations in total. These companies had strived for many years to establish the practice of home care in Argentina. Eventually, these efforts began to bear fruit and demand accelerated sharply. In the case of prolonged diseases of relatively low complexity, the low-cost value proposition home care providers offered gave them a competitive advantage that traditional hospitals could not surmount.

When we first began to consult with Sofía regarding her company in 2016, we asked her what she believed was the ideal growth rate for her business. What was the minimum size it needed to reach in order to ensure its survival once the industry transitioned to the maturity phase? Her response is not at issue. Rather, it was interesting to observe that the question made complete sense to her. It struck a nerve and helped her comprehend something she felt intuitively but could not articulate. In terms of growth, her company would have to respond to the present and future competitiveness of the industry in which it operates.

The answer to this question was not clear. To what extent could such a labor-intensive business be scaled up? The lack of qualified personnel slowed the potential for rapid scalability. Later, difficulties encountered in auditing these businesses raised doubts about the quality of services that would be offered under any large-scale operation. Despite these challenges, there were signs indicating that the largest companies with the largest market share would continue to benefit from certain advantages. Health insurance companies seemed to prefer to work with larger service suppliers in order to reduce administrative and coordination costs. These, in turn, could lead to consolidation in the home care industry.

Assuming widespread consolidation when the industry matured, the degree of pain the Home Healthcare Services could feel when it faced the developmental challenge would vary dramatically dependent on its competitive strength at the time. Sofía understood that growth in the meantime was paramount, but her parents lacked interest in fomenting it as they felt they no longer had the energy. Consequently, the company's attempts at sensemaking and working out what was going on were far from optimal.

Presenting this problem to the company was no easy task as its profitability was more than acceptable to the shareholding family. Also, embarking on a path of faster growth would have necessitated making significant changes based on the future achievement of a distant goal. The remoteness and uncertainty of a potentially challenging future, when considered in tandem with the comfort of the present, led the company to overemphasize the comfort of the present. Sofía wanted to grow the company at a faster rate and understood the risk of it remaining too small. Her family, however, was reluctant to undertake the organizational changes and professionalization that such growth would entail. They were unwilling to delegate day-to-day management responsibilities to experienced executives.

Let us consider further the stories of Steve Jobs, Bill Gates, and Sofía Nevares to highlight a few important points that must be taken into account. These decisions, which tend to be made when the industry is experiencing double-digit growth, define the degree of strategic freedom that the company will experience in the transition to industry maturity. Successful transition processes are designed during times when everything is running smoothly. This requires a special effort from management as the comfort of the present tends to obscure future challenges. That is why, during the calm before the storm, when a firm operates on "automatic pilot," it is fundamentally important to scan, analyze, and make sense of the broader environment.

The problem of determining the growth rate is in part a technical problem—that is, understanding the competitive isolation mechanisms that will foster industry-wide consolidation—but it is also an adaptive leadership problem. Leadership must motivate multiple stakeholders and factions within the company to coalesce around a goal whose achievement will require all parties to make concessions. Potential future scenarios, problems, and opportunities have to be taken into consideration as part of the sensemaking process.

In the next section, we analyze the technical elements that help alleviate the future developmental challenge. Next, we dive deeper into adaptive leadership problems to achieve this goal.

THE ROLE OF THE COMPETITIVE ISOLATION MECHANISMS

Throughout their history, companies build competitive isolation mechanisms that allow them to resist the imitation processes typical of all industries.[2] These mechanisms have been widely classified to help companies organize the formation of business strategies. We propose a classification that consists of dividing the possible competitive isolation mechanisms into two types according to whether they offer a differentiation advantage or a cost advantage.[3] This classification is useful as it helps focus attention on two fundamental variables of the income statement: revenues and costs.

Cost-based competitive isolating mechanisms are grounded in industry characteristics that allow for the reduction of average operating costs in a manner that is difficult to imitate.

The simplest examples are the economies of scale. When a fixed cost, such as advertising, in-house maintenance, or research and development, is maintained regardless of the number of products or services produced, companies with the largest market shares have cost advantages simply because of their larger size. These companies may also be more efficient, but economy of scale is an advantage enjoyed by the relatively large regardless of their organizational adroitness. Size per se is the source of the advantage. Assuming a fixed number of consumers in the short term, the largest companies will have cost advantages that result in a degree of competitive protection. When Coca-Cola launches a nationwide advertisement campaign, the company prorates that expenditure over the cost of its products, which have a share of market of almost 50 percent. To launch a similar nationwide campaign, a small competitor will have to spend a similar amount but will prorate the costs over much smaller product quantities. As a result, it will suffer a marked competitive cost disadvantage that is quite difficult to offset.

A concept similar to economies of scale is that of economies of scope. The mechanism differs in that advantage is obtained not as a result of the size of the company's market share but rather because a given amount of fixed costs are prorated across an array of products. In multiproduct companies, a certain portion of the company's costs will always be shared across product lines. As long as the additional complexity of maintaining multiple products does not create additional coordination costs that are not offset by the savings generated by cost sharing, the company will be advantaged by economies of scope. For instance, when Unilever distributes its wide range of brands to a supermarket, the company obtains cost advantages in comparison with a company that only distributes one or two products.

Economies of learning are similar to economies of scale but refer to cost reductions that emerge from experience. Learning economies exist if costs significantly drop as the company becomes a specialist and accumulates experience in a particular area. The main difference with scale economies is that learning economies do not stop at a certain level but persist in improving efficiency. Intel's semiconductor business in the 1970s represents one of the most remarkable examples of economies of learning. There are several other mechanisms of competitive isolation based on costs in addition to those already described, including exclusive or preferential access to strategic raw materials.

However, cost-based mechanisms often lack the degree of protective power provided by differentiation-based mechanisms. To the extent that a company can, in the mind of the consumer, achieve the differentiation of a product based on qualities other than its intrinsic characteristics, it will be in a highly enviable position. An example of this phenomenon is the taste test challenges between Coca-Cola and Pepsi in the soda business. When tasting each product blindfolded, regular Coca-Cola consumers were more likely to choose Pepsi than they were during their day-to-day purchasing decisions when subject to brand influence.

Switching costs are another typical demand-based mechanism. For example, changing the enterprise resource planning (ERP) systems a company uses is a painful process. This is why once a provider has installed its ERP system, it can expect the client to provide considerable protection from competition even if the services it offers are inferior to its rivals' services. If the provider has grown quickly enough, it will also likely benefit from protection for longer.

How do competitive isolating mechanisms, which we have described from the perspective of individual businesses, relate to the challenge of estimating the number of competitors the industry will allow when it reaches maturity? Generally, the type of industry will determine the type of competitive isolation mechanisms that firms can establish. Managers can determine where consolidation will occur and what type of companies will be in competition by analyzing the industry type. For example, if the company belongs to a digital platform industry, characterized by the existence of strong network externalities, consolidation will lead to the survival of one or, at most, two companies. For the case of consumer products, where brands are critical, the structure might have room for a dozen firms. Senior management teams need to assess the industry-level mechanisms of consolidation and ensure that their own companies are timely in meeting survival conditions.

These technical elements are the raw material for the senior management team discussions about the future. The strategic leadership problem that has to be addressed concerns the extent to which the company is prepared to face up to and survive the developmental challenge.

FOUR MORE YEARS

Our own understanding of this process became clearer in light of the experiences of one of our students. We first met Ignacio Marini at a strategic leadership program at the university where we teach. At the time, Ignacio was general manager of the Zona Austral of Nespresso, an operating unit of the Nestlé Group, whose head office was in Lausanne, Switzerland.[4] He was responsible for building the brand and capturing market share for their coffee products that were rapidly gaining favor with consumers after an initial struggle to find their place in the regional market. The products conveyed glamour and was perceived by consumers as being of high value.

For some time, Ignacio's company was the only one to offer this product in Latin America. Sales steadily increased, while Ignacio himself prospered as his career took an upward turn. In January 2017, however, for the first time, a competitor entered the market with a rival product, receiving significant coverage in regional newspapers. Ignacio felt compelled to carry out an exhaustive study of this new threat to his business. We went through the situation with him. Together, we acknowledged that consumption per capita in Latin America was still far below the levels of the Mediterranean area, which seemed to be the best reference market for anticipating what could happen in the market in which Ignacio was competing. After calculating some figures based on the product's diffusion rate and the potential of this particular product category, we estimated that the market would have at least four more years of very high growth rates.

The next step was to study the known competitive threats and the potential for other competitors to emerge in the market. As a result of its brand image, we concluded that the competitor featured in the newspapers would exert some pressure on prices but was not likely to make headway into Ignacio's target market in the medium term. We also concluded that other competitors could enter the market, with many international companies having sufficient capacity to do so. Nonetheless, assuming that some of these potential competitors would succeed eventually, most of them would not be able to match Ignacio's company for quite some time.

To complete the analysis, we assessed the company's internal context. Our main concern was understanding the kind of pressures the Zona Austral subsidiary might receive from the parent company as a result of the changes in the competitive environment. During that period, the parent company measured the performance of its regional subsidiaries with an algorithm that included sales data and profit margins. However, the head office was mostly concerned about the following year's sales target. Based on our discussion regarding the market and the company, we concluded that any new competitors in the market would serve to accelerate the development of this product category. In the short term, therefore, Ignacio's sales would continue to grow significantly. The impact that new competitors could have on prices, though, remained unclear, but it seemed unlikely that it would be necessary to reduce them any time soon.

After mulling over various aspects of the analysis, we concluded that the greatest threat Ignacio faced was market saturation—which we felt would occur within a few years. When that moment arrived, he would have to make major adjustments. By the time the market matured, however, the company would probably be well positioned to compete because it was already constructing the necessary competitive isolating barriers in the industry. In addition to leveraging strong brand differentiation, the company's relationships within the distribution channels was another key factor.

The situation seemed quite manageable. However, Ignacio's final conclusion, made only partly in jest, gave us pause. "So," he said, "I have about four years left before I need to start looking for a new job."

STRATEGIC LEADERSHIP IN TIMES OF BONANZA

Ironically, going through times of bonanza is probably one of the most challenging experiences a company can have. We are all subject to cognitive biases. One of these biases is giving inappropriate weight to time, in the sense that we are often held in thrall by the present, overvaluing its significance, and are often unrealistic in our expectations of the future. Such biases inform and shape how we run our businesses. We expect the good times to continue on and on and are taken by surprise when they come to an abrupt halt.

It is true that, during the current twenty-first century, we have witnessed accelerated change. Younger generations are no strangers to the rapid demise of once iconic companies. However, when the profit margin is high, growth is strong, and the company's competitive position is dominant, even the young succumb to the temptation to overestimate the duration of their success, drawing false comfort from an apparently continuous present.

When it is certain that only one competitor will remain in a given industry, placing a great deal of focus on the industry's and company's growth rates may be a waste of time—especially when there is a clear imperative for the company to grow as fast as possible. But in the vast majority of industries, a number of companies remain standing as their respective industry matures. This is why, during times of market expansion, a company's organizational imperative will often be to grow at a rate at least equal to the rate of the industry's growth. Indeed, this is the main lesson to be garnered from the examples in this chapter. However, companies in such circumstances should avoid developing a unique focus on growth during these periods, especially when it becomes clear that the company will face strong competition as the industry consolidates.

How do we know if a company is disproportionately focused on the short term? Cognitive biases manifest themselves within the organization in the form of incentive systems and formal structures. In a company whose focus is on obtaining the greatest percentage of market share possible, the formal structure creates static and insulated departments that seldom interact with other areas of the organization. Further, incentive systems tend to be very simple, rewarding only one variable—which is typically either sales or deliveries. During periods of boom or bonanza, it is incumbent on management to help the whole organization understand that this is merely the calm before the storm, that difficulties lie ahead and should be prepared for.

During the good times, a company's main challenge is to nurture and preserve its learning capacity. To that end, the senior management team must push the company to discuss the survival conditions for the long-term future. It is essential that the company secures enough share of the market to ensure its own survival. Equally important, however, is that it limits the creation of silos within the company as they are one of the major obstacles to corporate learning.

There is pressure on the senior management team during times of bonanza to start preparing the organization for those changes that will undoubtedly occur without severely constraining its ability to gain market share. The senior management team has to enhance the adaptation potential of the organization for what cannot be reasonably expected. As stated in the previous chapter, managers can expect that competitive rivalry will intensify, that per unit margins will fall, and that organizational complexity will increase to the extent that the company will grow in size and its product offering will be amplified.

THE RISK OF BEING WRONG ABOUT SUCCESS FACTORS

Managerial actions have consequences. Those consequences give us information with respect to whether those actions were taken correctly or were made in error. When a decision leads to a positive result it reinforces the interpretative models by which we view the world. When the outcome is negative, they become subject to stress. Success reinforces our self-esteem and self-confidence. Failure hurts because it makes us lose confidence in our own ability to face the future.

Because of this learning pattern, success is not always better than failure. In fact, as we have discussed in this chapter, there is risk in continued success. Generally, humans are afraid of being wrong, but of all the things a person can be wrong about, his or her understanding of error is likely to be at the top of the list. The ability to acknowledge and accept error is crucial to learning. It is neither a sign of intellectual inferiority nor of moral defect. Instead, it is the basis for some of the most honorable of human emotions and values, including empathy, optimism, imagination, conviction, and courage. Making mistakes is a fundamental part of how we learn and change. Thanks to errors and mistakes, we can evaluate and modify our understanding of the world and our place within it.

Unfortunately, this is not often the attitude organizational senior management teams adopt when they are confronted by error. To make matters worse, because errors can cause fear, the response is often to hold on desperately to what previously has had the appearance of success.

Times of bonanza may conceal death traps when a company's senior management team mistakenly associates the extent of recent success with the motives that led there. During these periods, a company grows and makes money heavily influenced by the fact of being in the right place at the right time. As this text has highlighted so far, the primary causal factor behind rapid growth with high profit margins is usually the decision to enter the industry at the right time and place.

Market share can be gained in times of high industry growth. This is a sign that something has been done right, although it is frequently the result of a decision to sacrifice profit margin for growth rather than the development of differentiating abilities. Again, general growth and profitability may follow specific decisions rather than superior organizational work and culture.

In boom times, it is crucial to recall the aphorism Socrates adopted as a maxim for life: "know thyself." Discovering a firm's source of success will be no trivial task and will demand personal magnanimity as well as sophisticated systemic work.

This is no trivial problem. When demand begins to dwindle and an organization's rate of growth starts to slow down, any management team that has failed to adequately identify the company's true success factors will likely formulate an incorrect response that ultimately may lead to failure. Avoidance of responsibility is typical in such circumstances. Blame is apportioned elsewhere: to the marketplace, to irrationally aggressive competitive moves, to clients' misunderstanding of the company's value, or to any number of other external culprits.

The temptation to avoid tasks and responsibilities, to identify and blame scapegoats is, sadly, very common as industries undergo change and organizations face up to transformational challenges. Generally, such behavior is characteristic of a management team that has incorrectly diagnosed the factors of the firm's success. Conversely, a team that has invested time and effort in assessing and understanding the origin of its growth and high profit margins during peaks in demand will be much better placed to adapt to change. For this reason, it is well worth appointing teams to assess a firm's success factors even if doing so carries its own challenges.

THE LEADERSHIP CHALLENGE WHEN
YOU HAVE LOST THE RACE

A company's fate is determined during an industry's development stage. Microsoft was an indisputable winner regarding personal computer operating systems. Android now appears to be leading the way with smartphone operating systems, while Apple remains competitive. However, the destiny of several competitors is to exit the industry. Blackberry and Microsoft lost the smartphone race, trying to sustain their own operating systems.

The systemic challenges that each firm will face differ depending on whether the company winds up in the winners' circle and, thereby, becomes a potential survivor of future transformational challenges or it slides into the group of contenders that are unlikely to survive when the industry matures. Similarly, companies that are neither clear winners nor losers will face other systemic challenges.

One of the difficulties in assessing whether a company is a winner is that measuring the potential future or existing competitive space in a mature industry is not subject to precision. Predicting a company's future survival in a competitive industry involves technical uncertainty, and also can be considered an adaptive challenge. Sailing into the eye of the storm has both technical and adaptive dimensions. Although there is certainty with respect to the storm's arrival, there is a great deal of uncertainty regarding its strength, the exact moment of its arrival, and, above all, how the crew will react on impact.

As the end of the expansion period approaches, often alarms begin to go off quickly. When sales drop and the pressure on profit margins increases, the entire company mobilizes. If this mobilization is delayed, however, the organization is most likely to suffer from task avoidance.

The potential reasons for a company's failure are many. It could have been a late entrant into the industry, or it might have adopted a business model that impeded growth at a proper rate. Whatever the case may be, there comes a time when companies realize that they are no longer competitive and their lack of viability in this specific industry is irreversible.

In such a scenario, a company has to plan its exit from the industry. From a purely strategic standpoint, the problem lies in determining the correct timing and the best mode in which to exit. Generally, preparing to exit means planning or arranging the company sale. Selling your company is a painful process that affects all parts of the organization equally. It entails changing your identity, preparing the organization to adopt that of the buyer. This is a task that has to be taken on primarily by the senior management team.

In the next chapter, we move back in time and consider the moment when established companies face disruption. We will focus on challenges similar to the one that General Motors has faced with Tesla's introduction of the electric car, or Walmart in response to Amazon's disruption of its marketplace.

CHAPTER 4

THE CREATIVE CHALLENGE

The creative challenge refers to the leadership dilemmas and business opportunities confronting a senior management team when an industry faces disruption. This chapter seeks to help senior management teams assess creative challenges to their companies and design the most effective adaptive interventions in response to these disruptive threats. Historical evidence demonstrates that if new technology or a radically new business model disrupts an industry in which you are already a successful player, the probability of your remaining a market leader is low. For this reason, we will look at, say, the leadership dilemmas encountered by General Motors as a result of the emergence of the electric car rather than Tesla's role in disrupting an established industry.

Fascination with the topic of disruption has increased steadily over the last decades among managers and in the business press, arguably for two contrasting reasons. On the one hand, the business community is experiencing unique growth opportunities made possible by technological changes and scalable business models. The concept of the *fourth industrial revolution* encapsulates this set of possibilities. On the other, failure rates are so high that frustration often increases when attempting to embrace these opportunities.

Still, some companies managed to evolve and succeed. IBM went through a dramatic change process and converted the business from a manufacturer of hardware to a service company that also has been at the cutting edge of the artificial intelligence sector with the launch of Watson. DuPont's first business was explosives. From there it moved to chemistry, and then to life sciences. Such a tremendous shift provides some hope regarding the organizational capacity to successfully embrace and adapt to disruption.

An organization faces the creative challenge when the threat of a potentially viable new business model puts into question the sustainability of the current one. We want to be clear on one point: having the intuition that your company will be disrupted is not in itself equivalent to facing the creative challenge. Today, for example, the executives of a slaughterhouse and meat-packing facility will be aware of the development of plant-based meat and of the potential future threat that could pose to their industry, but they have not yet been confronted by the creative challenge. For that to exist, the future and the change that will bring should feel near enough to generate immediate reactions and tensions within the organization. Uncertainty in such a scenario about what is likely to be the most viable business model going forward is precisely what should catalyze the intervention and action of the senior management team.

COMPETING FOR MEMORIES

There are few things as intrinsic to human nature as the desire to keep memories. Time slips through our fingers like dry sand. If we could, we would freeze certain moments to keep them alive forever. Since stopping time is impossible, we do what we can to store images of those moments. The development of the camera has provided us with a technology that has enabled us to fulfill this ambition, at least in part.

The evolution of photography and it associated technologies is inextricably linked with the story of Kodak. The company was founded as the Eastman Dry Plate Company in 1881 by George Eastman and Henry Strong, marking the birth of commercial photography. Later, the company became Eastman Kodak Company, a name that was commonly and widely abbreviated to Kodak.

The technical solution Eastman developed for capturing memories was based on three essential elements: film, paper, and development. A mechanical camera created images on a special film created by Eastman. Subsequently, there followed a development process that allowed for the transfer of the images to paper, where the photograph remained permanently.

Behind each step of the process, there was a value-adding activity, many involving chemical engineering, especially in connection with the production of quality film and the fine-tuning of manufacturing processes. Further, to reach consumers, it was necessary to have both a solid distribution network and to develop a strong brand. With time, Eastman Kodak's strong organizational capabilities in the areas of manufacturing, research, and development in chemical processes, distribution, and brand recognition became a strong competitive advantage that helped to gain and preserve market share. As a result, in 1960, Kodak held a 90 percent share of the global market.

The company's real business model did not lie with the camera, however, but the consumable goods used in conjunction with it. The camera served as an excuse to sell film and quality paper. Similarly, Gillette's business model was focused on replacement blades, not the shaving apparatus itself, and producers of photocopiers received higher returns on toner and paper products than they did on copiers. As such, for decades, Kodak concentrated its business on film and paper, developing outstanding skills and products.

The company's market dominance and competitive comfort lasted for several decades. Its first serious competitive threat arose in 1965 with the entrance of a low-cost competitor into the US market, the Fuji Photo Film Company. Kodak's executives refused to accept the presence of this competitor in the market and filed a lawsuit against Fuji for dumping (that is, selling at a loss), a suit that Kodak eventually won.

Fuji posed a significant threat but lacked the lethal force to overthrow the market leader. Kodak was Kodak, the father of photography, the synonym of memories, which is why, in 1980, it still held almost 80 percent of global market share. At the same time, another challenge to Kodak's dominance was emerging on the horizon: digital photography. With the digital image, the development of paper-based photographs became optional rather than necessary, as the images and the memories they captured could be viewed and shared on screens.

Fortunately, unlike Fuji's entrance into the market, which had taken Kodak by surprise, the digital threat was detected in time. After years of substantial technological investments, it was Eastman Kodak that patented the first digital camera in 1975. Just as the company had revolutionized photography in the late nineteenth century, it was well-equipped to lead the new revolution in photographic technology. Kodak enjoyed enormous prestige, as it owned one of the most recognized brands worldwide and had a reputation for quality.

The market waited expectantly, but the launch of Kodak's digital camera never arrived. Kodak held its digital camera patent for several years without seeming to do anything with it. Instead, in October 1981, it was a rival company, Sony, that announced it would introduce an all-electronic camera in 1983 designed to display still photographs on a television screen.[1] In doing so, Sony sounded the death knell for Kodak's long-established business model, signaling the start of a long and slow decline.

At the time, Sony was not a serious competitor as it was only taking baby steps with a camera that made use of analog television technology. Other companies, including Canon and Fuji, were trying to develop digital cameras, but they were far from achieving the quality of the film, paper, and development approach of Kodak. These products also were too expensive for the general public. Kodak, meanwhile, owned digital technology patents, benefited from a strong cash flow with which to finance research into new technology, and appeared able to depend on its strong brand when monetizing new products.

A familiar scenario was beginning to play out, though. The sound financial position in which the company found itself blinded its executives to the transformation that was necessary for Kodak to remain competitive in the long term. As the road ahead became bumpier, the Kodak board became increasingly reactive, hiring and firing one CEO after another. Successive turnaround failures were associated with the names of George Fisher, Daniel Carp, and Antonio Pérez, all of whom had indisputable talent and managerial skills.

As a tragic end to this story, Eastman Kodak filed for Chapter 11 bankruptcy protection in January 2012, seeking legal protection to restructure its debt obligations and business units. By September 2013, Kodak had emerged from its Chapter 11 status, but only after selling off many of its patents and core businesses, including its photographic film business. After more than 130 years, having dominated the photography market and developed the first digital camera, the company almost vanished from the world of memories. How was this possible? How did the undisputed and resource-rich industry leader encounter such catastrophic failure?

STATISTICS ON THE ENTREPRENEURIAL PROCESS

Failure after the launch of a new business stings the people behind the launches—especially the entrepreneurs who have enjoyed previous success when founding other businesses. The same can apply to the launch of new product lines, or, indeed, the failure to launch them, especially when the effect is to damage the rest of the business. It is useful to consider whether Kodak's failure was the result of organization-specific issues or whether it was indicative of an environment fraught with generalized challenges.

The process of developing a new enterprise is among the most frustrating in the business world. In its 2020 edition, *Small Business Statistics* reports that only 78.5 percent of small businesses survive their first year, while about half of companies manage to reach their fifth fiscal year, and one-third of all startups last a decade.[2] These results appear to be industry-agnostic. The US Census reports consistent results for survival rates of businesses across a variety of industries after five years of operation.[3] Although there is some heterogeneity between industrial sectors, in general, survival rates are markedly low.

There seems to be conclusive evidence that only a small number of new businesses survive in the long term. How do statistics vary when an established company launches a new business? Do the odds improve for ventures launched by successful businesspeople?

TABLE 4.1. Survival rate per industry, after five years of foundation

Industrial Segment	Percent Chance of Survival after 5 Years
Mining	51.3%
Manufacturing	48.4%
Services	47.6%
Wholesale and Agriculture	47.4%
Retail	41.1%
Finance, Insurance, and Real Estate	39.6%
Transport, Communications, and Utilities	39.4%
Construction	36.4%

WHEN SUCCESSFUL COMPANIES TRY TO REINVENT THEMSELVES

While studying innovation, we have come across an apparent paradox: it is often well-established, successful companies that are the first to develop prototypes of the disruptive technologies that eventually sink their own business. Despite this apparent head start on the competition, these companies appear to fail systematically when it comes to launching new ventures or business units based on revolutionary innovations. Consider, for example, that like Kodak, Polaroid also made great technological progress toward a digital camera. While Xerox, mindful of a potential drop in the use of paper-based copiers, was a pioneer in the development of key computing technologies, including the mouse, drag-and-drop functionality, and the graphic user interface that would eventually be popularized by Apple and Microsoft.

Sometimes, though, technological innovation serves as a distraction that draws the attention of senior leaders away from the more fundamental need to implement organizational change. Innovation means little to the bottom line if a business model capable of monetizing the new technology and providing sustained profitability does not support it.

So, if companies do not have too much difficulty in achieving technological discoveries and advancements, why do they fail so dramatically to reinvent themselves? According to business theorist Clayton Christensen,[4] the central dilemma innovators face is how to resolve the tension between what current clients demand and pay and what future clients will demand and pay. Current clients are usually very profitable but demanding. In contrast, future clients may demand less quality and greater simplicity than the company is accustomed to providing, yet these are the clients that illuminate the path to future growth.

In Kodak's case, its brand was associated with high-quality products, yet, even by the end of the 1990s, the digital camera still fell short of its exacting standards. Organizational resistance within Kodak may have arisen from a market- and customer-focused perspective. We encountered some of this resistance ourselves in 1998 when in conversation with a friend who is a professional photographer. He was adamant that digital photography would have no impact on the art he was able to create, in large part because it would be unable to match the quality he attained developing photographs in a darkroom. For him, the traditional practices were here to stay and digital photography would never be able to match them. How wrong he proved to be. How blinkered in his vision of the future.

For Kodak to have successfully entered the new digital world with competitive products would have required a fresh view and understanding of the customer. The key to the future was not in the hands of photography experts spending thousands of dollars on new equipment. Within only a few years, not only had consumers accepted photographs of lower quality taken with professional digital cameras, but technological advancement had also facilitated the use of the mobile phone to open up the world of stored memories further. To progress, to achieve success, it is necessary to detach yourself from the demands of current customers and to take the time to properly assess the industry's changing profile and the potential needs of future clients.

In the words of French novelist Marcel Proust, "the real voyage of discovery consists not in seeking new landscapes, but in having new eyes."[5] Renewing our eyes is, therefore, the first step to discover the opportunities that define how we must transition to the new world. To obtain a new vision of the world before us, we must constantly inform ourselves concerning new technologies and potential new business opportunities, and we must also maintain long-term dialogues with people who examine our shared realities from different angles and perspectives.

Consequently, a critical challenge for successful companies is to liberate themselves from the forces that prevent them from reinventing how they see and engage with the world around them. If established organizations could achieve this with regularity, they would have plenty of advantages over independent entrepreneurs, who themselves are often inhibited by the lack of resources and funding. An established organization with resources offers a good platform from which to launch new ventures. Often, though, such organizations are shackled by constraints that transform an apparent advantage into a liability.

THE TENSION BETWEEN TWO DISTINCT RATIONALES

To gain a better understanding of these constraints, compare and contrast the behaviors and actions of an entrepreneur with those of a general manager who works for a large company in a mature industry. At first glance, there are likely to be essential differences between the type of tasks they handle, what they consider to be their responsibilities, and their vision regarding their core business. In essence, though, each of them follows a rationale that is the polar opposite of the other. No wonder, then, that entrepreneurial initiatives bear so little fruit from within established organizations. Two different worldviews clash as the new and the disruptive are resisted, fought off like a virus by the organizational antibodies.

The entrepreneurial process is about discovery. The managerial process, in contrast, is much more about investing time in planning and routine processes to align the organization behind clear goals. Starting a new business involves a lot of trial and error, testing out ideas with clients, assessing their needs, and exploring the feasibility of unproven business models. There is a lot that is uncertain and unknown with the entrepreneurial approach, whereas, with traditional management, even when responding to opportunities, there is much that is known and familiar. The manager's task, more often than not, is focused on the transactional, on continuous improvement of processes, on setting objectives, on the identification and allocation of necessary resources, on the assignment of actions and deliverables, and on the assessment of progress.

Business academic and entrepreneurship expert Saras Sarasvathy has dedicated a significant proportion of her career to exploring the contrasting rationales that characterize entrepreneurs and executives of established companies. In her analysis, she describes these two rationales as being difficult but not impossible to reconcile. For Sarasvathy, the entrepreneur's rationale can be described as "effectual reasoning," whereas she refers to the managerial thinking associated with established firms as "causal reasoning."

Effectual reasoning involves employing a set of known resources in a world in which the result is unknown, undetermined, or uncertain. The entrepreneur is, in Sarasvathy's view, essentially an orchestrator of means or resources. The entrepreneur possesses a set of skills, materials, and relationships that enables them to fulfill certain business activity, but the overall result is uncertain and difficult to predict. For this reason, the role of an entrepreneur is to act and learn from the effects of their actions.

We learn through doing, in the moment, from both successes and failures. Our understanding deepens through iteration and refinement, with our new knowledge and experience guiding our future actions. Action is the first step toward sensemaking and generating new meaning. In other words, the explorer does not know what they are exploring until their exploration of it is complete. The quality and nature of an entrepreneur's actions, together with what they learn and discover as a consequence of them, contributes more to the success of their endeavor than their planning skills.

Causal reasoning, by contrast, involves employing known resources in a known world to reach a predetermined effect. Here, the objective is clear, and the cause-effect relationship that is in play is quite predictable. Because the terrain is well-known, a person following this rationale sets certain objectives and then tries to maximize the most efficient use of resources to achieve them. For instance, an executive may determine, with substantial precision, that if advertising spending is increased by a certain amount, sales will also increase by an equivalent percentage. Or they may estimate that a certain level of investment in order to adjust processes in one plant will have a proportional impact on the global efficiency of the business as a whole.

Both rationales are founded on different assumptions. These relate to the degree of knowledge that is required regarding the internal and external realities of the environment in which we want to operate. They also concern the effects of the actions we take. In an uncertain world, we can only control the way we search, and we cannot be beholden to preconceptions of where the road may lead. The only restriction we should place on the discovery process is that of affordable loss.

As a result, we need a different rationale and way of being than are required in a known world. However, this logic is not likely to find fertile ground among members of an organization's senior leadership team, as matters that are prevalent in the known world will dominate their thinking. They will be busy trying to optimize the competitive position of the current product portfolio, improving processes, or developing talent to improve the company's main income sources.

Both rationales are necessary: one for getting current businesses in order and the other for discovering future business opportunities. Paradoxically, they are mutually dependent, yet, at least in part, mutually exclusive, too. How, then, can the entrepreneurial impulse be permitted to flow inside an organization in which it is still necessary to organize, manage, and control the current business portfolio? Is there a way to explore unknown territory and apply known management processes so that exploration can proceed along the paths that make the most sense for the organization given its current state?

BEHIND THE NEWS

The news industry has undergone a massive transformation over the past few decades. Every newspaper across the globe had to deal with the impact of the internet on their business model in order to survive and grow. Newspapers adopted different strategies, with varying results. For example, *La Nación* in Argentina chose a route to address the challenges it faced different from, say, *USA Today* in North America.[6] This related, in particular, to how the organization was structured for learning.

The first words Angelica "Momi" Peralta Ramos said to us were, "When I met the internet I fell in love." Momi was a computer-systems engineer. Her passion was greater for information circuits than for programming, and she was more interested in communication than in coding. She began working at *La Nación* in 1994, ultimately inspired by the opportunity to push the delivery of news from paper to the internet. This became a personal passion as she diligently built a team that silently worked toward that goal. Momi had been recruited initially on a part-time basis by Ricardo Brom, working with him and the rest of their team to develop the first website for the paper.

At the time, the nascent World Wide Web was perceived as only a potential and distant threat, with newspapers, radio, and television the recognized standards for communicating with the public and monetizing current affairs. Founded in 1870, *La Nación* was a traditional, well-established newspaper for which a digitization program constituted a mammoth undertaking. This was exacerbated by the fact that, even as the threat posed by the web became increasingly palpable as the decade progressed, the paper's revenue model was healthy. Prestige and authority were vested in editors and journalists who were set in their ways. Momi, for her part, did not have any experience of the news business nor any legitimacy in the community that she was trying to mobilize to change.

Shortly after joining the newspaper, Momi produced a thirty-page proposal and presented it to the board. To her surprise, their response was substantially positive. Nonetheless, many within the company were not convinced, with people dismissing the web as a fad, questioning how they would maintain their advertising revenue, and wondering aloud about the wisdom of an initiative that was likely to discourage people from puchasing the paper when they could access its content online. Not only did senior managers voice their misgivings, but even supporters of a web-based platform could not readily quantify the value of implementing one. Meanwhile, the paper's journalists expressed existential discomfort with the speed of access and dissemination associated with the internet when the integrity of their profession depended on the methodical accumulation and cross-checking of facts.

The team, then, met resistance from all quarters and was inhibited further by a shortage of resources. The team who funded the first digital news page in *La Nación* included a tech-loving journalist and a few other individuals. Initially, management was only willing to approve these projects if they did not incur costs or take up time that employees normally dedicated to their regular work tasks. Despite this, the team achieved very significant advances in just a few years. The newspaper's home page became the most visited in Argentina. A decade after the creation of the digital unit, the project was an indisputable success. With one caveat: economically, the unit was not self-sufficient.

During Roberto's visits to *La Nación* in 2004, one thing that stood out for him was the grouping of the editorial desks on the fifth floor as a microcosm of the society on which they reported. There were politics, economics, sports, and agriculture, among others. It was fascinating to observe that the journalists somehow reflected in their clothing and style the subject matter about which they wrote. Even more noteworthy, though, was the fact that a glass barrier separated the digital unit from the rest of their colleagues, and that the age profile here was significantly younger than that of the "traditional" departments. The structure of this digital unit, though, mirrored that of the print teams on the other side of the glass.

One of the biggest problems the organization faced in switching from paper to digital was the impact on the newspaper's three principal sources of revenue. By the time we visited, unit sales had stagnated, advertisers were beginning to resist spending the same amount they had on paper-based advertisements, and classifieds were moving to a wholly digital format. The design and organization of the digital unit, far from enabling it to shadow the organization's print colleagues, in fact served to limit it in its abilities to respond to market changes and shifting customer requirements. The unit could not adapt and grow as it needed to.

In 2005, *La Nación* decided to make drastic changes to the way it approached digital. The company purchased 19.27 percent of DeRemate.com, an online auction platform that was popular across Latin America. As part of this transaction, Guido Grinbaum, the founder of DeRemate.com, joined the ranks of *La Nación*. Like Momi, Grinbaum had an entrepreneurial mindset and also brought significant knowledge and experience of e-commerce to the paper's digital team.

Encouraged by Grinbaum, *La Nación* developed a variety of business units connected with activities previously associated with the paper but now confronted with specialist competitors in several emergent industries. The online journal continues to compete for advertising space with large search engines. Classifieds became a physically separate e-commerce platform under the name of DRIDCO. In addition, the journal developed a membership scheme, offering subscribers discounts at various restaurants and retail outlets. The effect of the membership scheme was that, for a short period, until 2013, there was a marginal increase in newspaper sales, after which they started to decline again.

Generally, though, despite being the first Argentinean periodical to launch a digital platform, *La Nación* was still struggling to turn a profit. The new business units themselves might have enjoyed success, but they were separated physically and organizationally from the rest of the company.

TRANSITIONING TO THE NEW WORLD FROM THE PERSPECTIVE OF THE ORGANIZATION

The ability to transition to new market realities, and the pace at which this transition happens, is largely dependent on the company in question having the relevant competencies. The organization also needs to be able to demonstrate a willingness to change its business model in order to stay relevant. It has to bridge the gap between old practices and new necessities, and it has to adapt the business model to different revenue streams.

General Motors, Ford, and Toyota, for example, traditionally received their revenues from selling cars and spare parts. In the United States, the typical vehicle remains parked 95 percent of the time; the average UK car is parked 96.5 percent of the time, even higher than Shoup's US estimate.[7] With the disruption of electric and autonomous vehicles, this might significantly change. The widespread embrace of shared, autonomous electric vehicles, deployed in a way that complements growing transit systems and improved walking and biking infrastructure, can offer an efficient transportation solution that's more affordable than car ownership for everyone. Therefore, carmakers will need to shift their business models from selling cars and repairing them to renting them—they will need to stop being product-oriented companies and move toward being service-oriented ones.

Polaroid and Kodak had to shift from a focus on photographic consumables to digital equipment as their principal source of revenue. Similarly, the newspaper industry has had to move from paper products to digital platforms as a way of deriving income from advertising, classifieds, and paywall content. Even then, newspapers face stiff competition from the likes of Google across the entire spectrum of e-commerce.

Leaders can deal with this challenge through any number of approaches. Dividing or making more flexible the organizational structure is a common response. This is based on the sound principle that the company has to avoid causal managerial thinking from suffocating any entrepreneurial endeavor. This necessarily gives rise to the possibility that new business units are separated from the rest of the organization both in a physical and structural sense. However, with a wall between new and traditional business units, how can a company ensure that these different areas of the organization do not grow so differently from one another that their future integration may prove impossible?

The answer is all but self-evident. The difficulty resides in ascertaining the appropriate level of integration. The more integrated the new business with the traditional structure, the easier it will be for the new organization to preserve its original identity. However, the more integrated the unit, the more difficulties it will encounter when exploring and exploiting new opportunities. Entrepreneurship is, above all else, knowing how to seek out such opportunities, to experiment, and to learn. Separating those who know how to look from those who know how to manage and organize makes it more likely that an embryonic organization will emerge that will eventually evolve into something distinct from the parent company.

One answer to the problem lies in the formal organizational structure. Robert Burgelman of Stanford University focused on this aspect of the problem during the 1980s. His suggestion was simple: the greater the need for new competencies and capabilities, the greater the need to create a structure that separates new business units from established ones. The same logic applies to the strategic relevance of new projects. The more radical the innovation, and the greater the impact it will have, the more we must protect the embryonic venture by separating it from the existing organizational structure. Such an approach also has an effect on assessment and control systems. Organizational routines are designed to improve familiar processes and tasks. Given the unknown dimension of new initiatives, such routines are often unsuited to them and can even have an inhibiting effect on them.

It should be acknowledged, though, that structural separation does not itself get to the heart of the problem. The objective is not to develop a new venture within the organization but, instead, to ensure the company's overall survival by going through a process of creative transformation. This will lead the organization from the known to the unknown, often moving away from the very strengths on which its competitive advantage were founded.

It can be the case, in fact, that the separation of a new business from its parent company is not be the most advantageous option. In contrast to the strategy of *La Nación*, which launched its digital newspaper in a manner that was integrated with the paper edition's editorial desks, *USA Today* opted for a complete separation of the physical and formal structures. *USA Today*'s digital paper was independent of the paper edition and its staff was located in a separate building, with the aim of guaranteeing autonomy. The management and journalists of the online newspaper did not face the same pressures as those working on the paper edition. They had total liberty to deal with the challenges of the new business as they best saw fit, and with this freedom they were able to grow the digital business rapidly and with considerable success. However, when the dot.com bubble burst in 2001, the digital unit began to encounter serious financial problems, as its revenue model was still not capable of supporting its expenditures. Following a review, *USA Today* sought to integrate its digital platform back into its core business.

PREPARING FOR THE ADAPTIVE INTERVENTION

The definition of the level of structural separation is a necessary condition dimension when addressing the creative challenge. But staying at this level can be a deadly trap, a calm surface hiding powerful waters that take everything in its path. The structure is just the holding environment for learning to begin. However, the senior management team will need to activate organizational energy to transform the entire organization. In the next chapter, we describe the process of mobilizing the organization to face the creative challenge.

CHAPTER 5

NAVIGATING THE CREATIVE CHALLENGE

SALIENT ASPECTS OF THE CREATIVE CHALLENGE

The creative challenge is the most difficult that an organization can face. There is uncertainty no matter which aspect of it you address. Which sources of income will disappear? How will we compensate for their loss? What will be our future business model? What new competencies do we require? Will our current expertise continue to add value? Do we have the right talent to see us through? Will our organizational identity change? These are all questions with no easy or known answers. No internal or external authority can readily solve them. Instead, a period of questioning and discomfort has to be endured, as solutions are sought and tested. These questions generate a high level of tension, and a natural response for many teams is evade or ignore them.

Consider, again, the newspaper industry. A traditional, hard-copy newspaper used to depend on three principal sources of revenue: sales of individual papers, print advertising, and classified advertisements. For many newspapers, these revenue sources were divided approximately into thirds. At the most basic level, the removal of the need to publish on paper meant significant savings in printing and distribution. More fundamentally, though, digitization changed the industry's business model, destroying long-established sources of revenue. At *La Nación*, the savings equaled about one-third of the company's revenue. Unfortunately, however, the switch from paper to digital also meant losing two-thirds of the company's historic sources of revenue owing to the disappearance of paper sales and the migration of classified advertisements to other digital formats. As digitization took hold across the industry, newspapers were having to identify new ventures that would compensate for the missing third from their old revenue streams.

When preparing for a creative challenge, a senior management team will need to consider how the industry's business model generates revenue now and to plan for how it will continue to do so in the future. To help with this, a map of the different factions involved can be used to anticipate pressures that are likely to be placed on the company's leadership. Factions are stakeholder groups or major players who are involved in or affected by the challenge. To create a faction map, the company needs to identify what are each faction's values, why they care about a particular issue, and what losses each faction might experience as the company attempts to make progress on the creative challenge. The map is an essential tool when navigating a creative challenge, helping identify possible ways forward as well as potential blockages. For example, expertise associated with established practice can inhibit change and organizational learning. Identifying where expertise lies under the current business model, therefore, is essential. Among the most critical voices to be heard are those of existing and potential clients. It is very probable that current client behavior will point the way toward likely pockets of resistance to the new business model within the organization. The commercial department's capabilities tend to mirror current customers' demands. This, however, may not be the case in relation to new and potential customers. An in-depth client analysis will provide insights about where to look and what to pay attention to.

There is something paradoxical about undertaking a *conflictual interpretation* during a creative challenge. While creative challenges are among the most dangerous for organizations, the level of internal tension tends to be relatively low when they occur. This is especially the case in the very early days, when an industry is starting the process of radical transformation. Consequently, the temptation to engage in work avoidance is much higher than in other leadership challenges. Ronald Heifetz, Alexander Grashow, and Marty Linsky define work avoidance as the conscious or unconscious patterns in a social system that distract people's attention or displace responsibility in order to restore social equilibrium at the cost of progress in meeting an adaptive challenge.[1] The adaptive creative challenge is to discover and develop the future business model. Yet work avoidance will discourage this experimentation. This manifests itself in different forms, as we shall explore.

Brian Arthur explains the type of uncertainty companies have to navigate in the creative challenge.[2] To do so, he builds on a casino analogy.

> Imagine you are milling about in a large casino with senior figures from high tech. At one table a game is starting called Multimedia. At another is a game known as Web Services. There are many such tables. You sit at one.
>
> "How much to play?"
>
> "Three billion," the croupier replies.
>
> "Who'll be playing?"
>
> "We won't know until they show up," she replies. "They will emerge as the game unfolds."
>
> "What are the odds of winning?"
>
> "We can't say," respond the croupier. "Do you still want to play?"

When the payout, the rules, and the competitors are unknown, typical work avoidance behavior is to interpret the problem as one that we know how to solve. This is true to such a degree that Karl Weick has said that we only see a problem when we think we can resolve it.[3] Given that very few people have an inkling of what can be done when facing a creative challenge, the tendency for work avoidance is at its highest.

Sometimes avoidance manifests itself as disengagement or the postponement of critical discussion. This type of avoidance mechanism is very seductive, especially when there is the perception of abundant time. In 1976, any mention of the digital camera brought up notions of a far-off world, even though the technology existed at the time to produce certain types of digital images. This brings us to another paradox seen in creative challenges: individuals who have the best understanding of the path the industry needs to follow in order to change effectively are often those with the least amount of organizational authority, formal or otherwise. This dynamic is not likely to be seen in developmental challenges. For this reason, organizations are often tempted during creative challenges to engage in another avoidance behavior: the marginalization of whomever brings up the problem.

The tendency toward generalization rather than specificity is another avoidance mechanism. A statement suggesting that "technology is going to affect us" is as true and obvious as it is useless and unproductive, adding nothing to the discussion. The productive tension needed to mobilize change processes comes in conversations about details, not from sweeping universalities. In general, people are not willing to risk their interests for abstract concepts.

Designing *adaptive interventions* will require fighting against typical work avoidance temptations and behaviors. The creative challenge is at its height when the critical processes on which the current business is based begin to be changed or replaced and when the client does not know what it will want exactly in the new world. The business remains as if it were suspended in an abyss without reference points. As the business model changes, the organization tends to suffer from an identity crisis. Reactively, the organization will try to change everything except factors that are perceived as affecting organizational identity. Without clear guidelines instructing all parties regarding the search for a solution to the problem of the business model, the different factions will close their ranks against one another's positions.

The organization's formal leadership should design the correct environments for addressing the fundamental questions and sustaining productive tension. Sometimes it is necessary to make changes to the formal structure, creating separate spaces for experimentation and filling them with employees who are convinced that change is the first step in an inevitable process. The challenge then is to later mobilize the whole organization to move toward the new destination point. On occasion, strategic planning can be useful for this, but only once fundamental uncertainties about the future have become clearer. The creation of multifunctional groups also can be helpful. These groups are likely to generate high levels of tension among their participants. To ensure the search and integration processes are carried forward, the support of those in the organization with formal authority is critical. Of course, the senior leadership should abstain from the temptation to offer and sell solutions to the organization. In any event, it is highly unlikely that they will be in possession of a silver bullet that will resolve all the problems the organization faces.

To ensure the effectiveness of leadership interventions, we recommend the development of four complementary actions. First, senior management teams should increase the sense of urgency, awakening the organization. Second, they should establish the organizational context and create a new team with a license to experiment. Third, they should work intensively at maintaining the holding environment while keeping adequate levels of productive tension. Finally, they should emphasize the organizational purpose to guide the discovery process.

We recommend these four steps following the adaptive leadership guidelines. However, the process has some overlap with others that offer an alternative perspective, such as the dual-operating-system model advocated by John Kotter in *Accelerate*.[4]

AWAKEN THE ORGANIZATION

It is the dead of the night in the middle of winter. Outside the house, the thermometer reads -5°C. The heating system maintains a pleasant temperature inside the building. Nonetheless, getting out of bed, one's body takes note of the cold. The alarm clock sounds at five thirty in the morning. Sunday night's rest was intermittent and broken, a portent of the problems awaiting us on Monday morning. Despite our reticence, we must get out of bed and face the day.

What is it that motivates us to start the working day? There is probably very little logic or reason involved in this. Many people would respond that it is simply a matter of habit. But emotions, whether they are good or bad, are what drive us to get up. The alarm sounds and alters our emotional state while our brain is still attempting to understand what is going on.

When dealing with greater challenges, emotions play an essential role. They are the key to waking the organization from its drowsy status quo, enabling it to make adjustments for the future. They will lead, pull, or inhibit the action required by the organization to discover a sustainable mode of future survival.

When designing the first adaptive interventions to address the creative challenge, it can be very useful to keep in mind the analogy of getting out of bed. It is like setting off the alarm clock over and over again, without any urgency but with a tolerable cadence.

The alarm clock metaphor can be applied in many ways. It is the industry specialist who familiarizes us with the latest trends. It is the scientist who pushes us to the very limits of our imagination as they outline new discoveries and developments. It is the successful entrepreneur from overseas who is brought in to explain how business is changing. It is the special management excursion designed to force participants out of their comfort zones. It is the youthful junior employee invited into the boardroom to challenge management's thinking and assumptions.

All these examples present first steps on a journey of discovery, a move toward a new world requiring different processes, habits, and behaviors. The alarm clock is a catalyst, an awakening. What follows requires open-mindedness, expansion, divergence, and discussion before any consensus is reached about destination. Then transformation itself can begin.

DESIGN INITIAL STEPS TO DISCOVERY

The discovery phase is characterized by small projects and experiments, adaptive interventions that trigger and build on the initial awakening. Here it is important to consider three dimensions: the *team*, mechanisms to evaluate *advancements*, and *structural protection*.

Interventions designed to awaken the organization help leadership identify the possible actors on which the discovery process can rely on for support, pushing forward with new exploratory projects. These are led by *teams* that report directly to senior management, although it is probable that the senior management team will not get directly involved in carrying these projects forward, principally because the traditional business must be maintained and cared for. From an adaptive standpoint, mobilizing change through alarm clocks generates enough tension so that the organization of these teams can happen organically. The projects will have a systemic impact and will benefit from the richness of diverse perspectives and talents. It is advisable, therefore, to assemble the project teams from people who previously have been involved in a variety of different functions across the organization, avoiding the dominance of a single, strong personality.

The greater the organization's commitment to take on the challenges that disruption has brought, the more uncertainty there is concerning the processes it will apply in doing so. Therefore, designing measures to evaluate *advancement* is crucial. Leaders must resist the temptation to use the same tools to measure success on these discovery projects as are used for traditional initiatives. However, there must be some tools to ensure that projects do not become erratic brainstorming think tanks that burn through company resources without showing results. This is a delicate dance between three values that are in tension: creativity, effectiveness, and efficiency.

For this reason, companies should establish evaluative mechanisms for measuring creative progress and should create mechanisms for measuring—as secondary interests—effectiveness and efficiency. Given that the organization at this point is immersed in a discovery process, management would be wise to request the use of semistructured criteria so that the process does not become anarchic.

Finally, it will be necessary to establish adequate *structural protection*, or *structural separation*, for new projects. This is particularly important concerning evaluation and control mechanisms used for established business operations. If the new discovery units are adequately protected, and their team reports to senior management, any incursion from the organization's traditional control centers on their processes is redundant and distracting and may well be a principal cause for their failure.

SUSTAIN THE BALANCE BETWEEN PRODUCTIVE TENSION AND A HOLDING ENVIRONMENT

All organizational learning processes require both productive tension and a holding environment. This is because organizational learning requires the factoring in of losses. For Heifetz, Grashow, and Linsky, a holding environment is a virtual space formed by a network of relationships within which individuals can, without falling victim to work avoidance behaviors, pose and consider difficult and sometimes conflicting questions. Holding environments are useful for channeling energy toward conflict resolution, avoiding descent into irrationally passionate confrontation.

During the creative challenge, productive tension and the holding environment take a very particular form. In the previous section, we outlined different elements for both. As the discovery process advances, senior management teams must simultaneously sustain and develop in different ways the holding environment as well as keep the levels of organizational tension at a productive level.

There are different methods by which a holding environment can be created and sustained. The holding environment can take the form of clearly defined processes, protocols, the use of prototypes, scoping parameters for a new business model, evaluation procedures, and deadlines. This typically involves free experimentation and the expectation of failure. They are means by which to confirm, verify, and control organizational progress. The conviction of those in authority is, most probably, the essential holding environment during this process. Inevitably, multiple initiatives will fail before a new path is found.

In the learning environments we see in connection with creative challenges, there are few factors that are as necessary as nurturing a stable holding environment to allow for the organization to "let go" and assume its losses. This holding environment will allow for the creation of a new shared language. Indeed, the act of giving new names to things that surround the organization helps to establish context and understanding of its competitive position. Achieving this shared language is, in fact, intrinsic to the creative challenge. It is a matter of building shared stories that unite the organization and facilitate its mobilization toward the future.

Karl Weick illustrates how these tensions function in a story involving a small military unit training in the Swiss Alps.[5] They were not familiar with the terrain, and it began to snow. The storm lasted two days. The unit realized it was lost. They were hungry and cold, and suffering and panic was evident until a young soldier found a map in his pocket. Everyone crowded around trying to figure out where they were and how they could get out. They calmed down, located themselves, and plotted a route back to their base. They pitched camp, lasted out the snowstorm, and moved into action. Of course, they did not always hit the landmarks they thought they would, and their journey back involved still more sensemaking. They received help from villagers along the way and shifted their path when faced with obstacles. When they reached base camp, they discovered that the map they had been using was a map of the Pyrenees and not the Alps. The moral of the story? When you are tired, cold, hungry, and scared, any old map will do. The map provided a sort of holding environment that allowed the team to move forward.

A holding environment has multiple dimensions. Conviction of authority is among these. However, in the context of creative challenges, an organization's formal authority figures are very probably not among those who are most likely to point the organization toward the right future. Therefore, the most important leadership behavior in learning processes designed to confront creative transitional challenges is to demonstrate conviction with respect to the direction of the search, rather than to provide answers.

EMPHASIZE ORGANIZATIONAL PURPOSE AND BOUNDARY EXPANSION

Why exactly do creative transitional challenges often descend into tragedy? Typically, two reasons present themselves simultaneously. The first is that the prevalent industrial business model becomes obsolete. The second is a patent inability to learn. We may well see tragedies in other types of leadership challenges, but they will be distinct from the tragedies associated with creative challenges. The key to survival and the greatest asset in these circumstances is the ability to learn. Because new business paradigms stretch organizational competencies to the limit, no other leadership challenge requires a greater capacity to learn.

The dilemma the creative challenge poses is how to secure the long-term survival of organizations, enduring beyond the limitations of the economic context for which they were designed. This is achieved through an anchor in the form of organizational purpose, the very reason for which the company exists. During creative challenges, organizational purpose serves as a fundamental cornerstone. Creation is always a social process. Existence in an organization is a process of shared meaning between its members. This is the development of a shared language. During the creative process, this edification is an open search with minimal levels of certainty and very few reference points or benchmarks. As a result, the organization's anchor becomes of utmost importance: a place on which to rest and secure this open search for new paradigms amid the high levels of uncertainty affecting the organization.

Profound questions arise in the mind of anyone who begins the process of leading an organization to a fundamentally different destination than the one originally envisaged and designed by its creators. It is easy to begin questioning why we are doing this, wondering why we should subject the organization to such severe levels of tension, asking whether a more prudent course of action would be to break the company up, give every stakeholder what is rightfully theirs, and start over.

Would it have been a better course of action for Kodak to dispose of its assets when they still retained value? It might have been preferable to the gradual bleeding out the company eventually experienced. This gets to the nub of the most difficult question to answer when facing a creative challenge. The stakeholders of the organization should look to the organizational purpose for guidance. It is the final measuring stick by which we can assess up to what point setting out on a risk-strewn path is worth the trouble.

The need to emphasize organizational purpose is also critical when we consider another aspect of the creative challenge: most organizations lack the capability necessary to explore. As such, they have to overcome the long-established tendency to do everything in-house. During the discovery process, alliances are fundamental both to success and the management of failure.

IS THE NEWS INDUSTRY STILL IN THE CREATIVE CHALLENGE?

The news industry faced a radical transformation with the advent of the World Wide Web in the late 1980s. It took around twenty years for incumbents to find a viable business model. However, during the last decade, the industry has been confronted by what appears to be a new revolution. Is this a new creative challenge?

The Guardian, for example, underwent similar changes to those experienced by *USA Today* and *La Nación*. However, during the last decade, its business model has changed dramatically, shifting from digital as a complement to paper-based news services to digital as the center of all news activities. This has led to changes in the way news reporters and editors operate as well as a broadening of who and how people contribute content, incorporating social media, comments sections, interactive content, photographic and video contributions by both the public and professionals, and analysis by data scientists.

The result of this shift has been the expansion of the geographic boundaries of the company. Traditionally, news tended to be located in specific regions or countries. However, the digital context tends to be much more global due to the ease of communicating it. In addition to its UK base, the organization has now a significant presence in Australia and the United States and, in 2019, began to expand its coverage in New Zealand as well.

The question remains, though, of whether *The Guardian* is in the midst of a creative challenge or has progressed already to traditional strategic management. The transition to a digital-first modus operandi is certainly indicative of a company dealing with a creative challenge. However, the worldwide scaling of an organizational business model is more suggestive of a traditional growth strategy. It is our view, therefore, that the recent experiences of *The Guardian* and other news organizations point to an industry accelerating growth before facing its next developmental challenge.

BRIEF GUIDE
to Spotting and Responding
to Creative Challenge

SCAN THE EXTERNAL ENVIRONMENT
Assess the Likelihood of Your Industry Being Disrupted

The likelihood of disruption increases if you compete in a mature industry and it has experienced only incremental innovation in recent times. Competitive positions are stable, and new entrants have difficulty posing any threat to incumbents. Customers have expert knowledge of your product. The way of doing business has not changed for years and most recent entrants have followed a niche strategy.

Test Out Your Intuition by Monitoring Your
Competitors' Response to Media Coverage

The likelihood of disruption increases when the media reports on new technologies that will affect your industry. Increasingly, there is news of industry outsiders testing radically different business models that threaten the established ones. Many of the existing competitors in the market suffer paralysis, unable to act, and lacking clarity about solutions and business models that will be sustainable in the long term. Some, however, do start to experiment.

SCAN THE INTERNAL ENVIRONMENT— MAKE INTERPRETATIONS—MOBILIZE

Determine the Recurrent Type of Work Avoidance

There are a few individuals who perceive the reality of the competitive threat, but they have enormous difficulties in supporting their arguments. The threat is viewed as something that will be realized only in the distant future. Temptation to engage in work avoidance is also at its height, and comments such as "that will never happen" and "there will always be clients willing to pay for our products" may be heard throughout the company.

The manifestation of disruption brings home the impact on the corporate balance sheet over the next five years. Everywhere can be seen people seeking solutions while still blinkered by the constraints of the old business model and ways of working.

Detect Expert Bias

Company experts often impede any significant discussion about the future. Experts use technical jargon and specifications, making it difficult to sustain a productive dialogue. There are often difficulties understanding how the company's current competitive advantages can support the new business.

Assess the Likely Effect of Losses across the Workforce

The loss of capacity is at its height when a competitive threat materializes. As it is uncomfortable to feel incompetent, different organization members hide their insecurity behind different types of emotional reactions and work avoidance mechanisms. Those that are at the end of their career view it with less anxiety than mid-career managers. Young employees usually face the lowest levels of loss, but mid-career managers face the highest ones.

Build the Holding Environment to Start Mobilizing the System

The higher the threat, the more important holding environments become. Share, as a management team, your own incompetence and show your willingness and determination to learn. This will create a safer atmosphere for people to express their fears and discuss areas of incompetence. When we all acknowledge the need to learn, incompetence is no longer a burden, and we are open to share our struggles, ask for help, and support others. The COVID pandemic was a real-life experiment where most organizations experienced this dynamic relative to digital capabilities. Therefore, the learning processes accelerated at unprecedented rates. A senior professor of an Ivy League business school told us, "in one semester, we experienced a transformation we anticipated would take us a decade."

Speed Up Learning Processes

Develop organized environments for controlled experimentation. Cultivate environments of productive tension. Use them as platforms from which learning from small-scale initiatives can be disseminated to the rest of the organization. If disruption is still at an initial stage, manage environments containing productive tension separately from the structure of the organization.

Monitor Progress

Senior management must resist the temptation to use the same tools to measure success on these discovery projects as are used for traditional initiatives. However, there must be some tools to ensure that projects do not become erratic brainstorming think tanks that burn through company resources without showing results. This is a delicate dance between three values that are in tension: creativity, effectiveness, and efficiency.

Connect to Organizational Purpose

To facilitate future integration, reinforce the company's relationship with its organizational purpose. Inevitably, the creative challenge places organizational identity in stress. Make it a topic of discussion. The holding environment you have created will facilitate these conflicting but necessary conversations.

CHAPTER 6

THE EMERGENCY CHALLENGE

The emergency challenge refers to the leadership dilemmas and business opportunities confronting a senior management team when a country enters into recession. It is just a matter of time before your country's economy will enter into a period of recession. It may be difficult to anticipate its depth and severity, but it will harm corporations. Every year the number of companies that declare bankruptcy in the United States is around half a million, an already vast figure that rises significantly the year after a recession begins. Small firms suffer disproportionately more, but large firms also experience the adverse effects of a macroeconomic contraction.

The increase in the level of postrecession bankruptcy and strategic damage, while not wholly unexpected, given what has happened in the past, still manages to take people by surprise. CEOs are well aware that, sooner or later, their organizations will have to navigate a recession and that they could and should prepare for it. However, it seems that they systematically fail to prepare their companies for these turbulent periods.

The average tenure of a CEO in developed and emerging economies is six to seven years.[1] In a seventy-five-year period, from the end of World Word II until February 2020, the United States has experienced eleven economic recessions. On average, they have lasted 11.1 months, according to the official scorekeepers at the National Bureau of Economic Research. The shortest was over in just six months (1980) while the longest lasted eighteen months (2007–9).[2]

In some other developed countries, such as New Zealand, the recession rate has been higher, while most emerging economies have been affected more frequently and with greater severity. The odds that while in office a CEO will not encounter an economic downturn in the United States or in overseas subsidiaries are pretty low.

While statistics indicate that company failures increase during recessions, there are also many stories of successful recession management. These include diverse types of organizations with markedly different competitive situations. It seems that every company can gain from recessions and macroeconomic recoveries, regardless of their competitive position in their given industry.

Few domestic Spanish firms were prospering during the global financial crisis that started in 2007. Mercadona was one of the few exceptions. Its market share grew from 23.3 percent in 2008 to 24.2 percent in 2009, reinforcing a trend that had been established a decade before.[3] Mercadona, leveraging a cost-based structure and simplified operations, used the recession to surpass Carrefour's competitive position.

The year 2002 was a dramatic one for Argentineans: the gross domestic product (GDP) contracted 11 percent, with a 20 percent contraction in the first quarter of the year. Danone, the French dairy foods conglomerate, consolidated its leadership position in Argentina in the decade that followed the country's 2002 economic crisis, while several competitors exited the industry. Between 2002 and 2008, Danone's market share in dairy products increased from 66 percent to 77 percent, while its share of the bottled water market rose from 52 percent to 57 percent.[4]

The US automotive industry remembers the years 2008–9 as painful ones, with sales dropping almost 30 percent. In addition, GM and Ford continued their market share loss during this period. However, news was not so bad for Hyundai: it jumped from a 2.9 percent market share in 2007 to 4.6 percent in 2010, sustaining its position the following year and on until at least 2016, when it started to decrease slightly. This was not the consequence of a technology breakthrough. It was simply the result of a tenacious strategy that Hyundai followed for years and bore success during the 2007–9 macroeconomic meltdown. Hyundai's years of work on cost and quality bore outstanding results during and after the great recession.

History repeats itself when we consider businesses that were established within tough macroeconomic periods. Thomas Edison founded General Electric during the 1873 US recession. Charles and Joseph Revlon, together with Charles Lachman, founded Revlon, the famous cosmetic firm, in 1932, at the end of the Great Depression. The luxury hotel chain Hyatt Park was founded in 1957, at the beginning of another US recession that lasted for two years. Bill Gates quit pursuing higher education during the 1973 recession to create Microsoft. Frederick Smith launched FedEx in the same year.

These two chapters are about how to mobilize your organization to take advantage of recessions. We provide tips about how to prepare your company not only to alleviate the adverse effects of the next recession but also to enhance its current competitive position. To achieve this goal, managers need to recognize how the recession virus infects profit and loss statements. They also need to understand how to mobilize the organization to prepare for and navigate the economic downturns. In other words, they need to master the emergency challenge.

A COLOMBIAN-AMERICAN IN ARGENTINA

What would have happened if Ray Kroc, the man who expanded the McDonald's empire, had selected Argentina for developing his ideas? We mention Argentina because it is hard to find a nation that has experienced more macroeconomic recessions and recoveries during the last half century. We have no answer to this question; Ray Kroc decided to build on foundations already established by the McDonald brothers in California. Eventually, however, another exemplary manager, Woods Staton, took up the mantle and began to build an empire in and from Argentina, based on the McDonald's brand and business model.

The first time Roberto visited Staton, they met at the Olivos headquarters of Arcos Dorados[5] in the Greater Buenos Aires metro area. What most caught his attention about him was the energy he communicated through his handshake. A simple handshake suggested the force of a whirlwind, sweeping up everything in its path.

Staton is from a family of businessmen. His grandfather, Albert, was a Coca-Cola executive who later founded the world's largest Coca-Cola bottler, with a presence in Colombia, Mexico, and several other Latin American countries. Staton, having often traveled with his grandfather on business trips, fulfilled a personal dream when he joined the family enterprise in the United States. Soon, though, he was drawn to venture further afield as he sought to develop his career more.

What was he to do? He analyzed the market and his attention was captured by McDonald's, whose business model at the time was the envy of the corporate world. Staton visited the corporate headquarters in Illinois, offering to open franchises in Colombia, a place that was especially dear to him and where he had experience and contacts. But luck did not seem to favor his plans. McDonald's declined to pursue the Colombia option, advising him to seek alternative sites.

Shocked by this rejection, Staton took another look at the map. He didn't know where to go, but in the middle of a conversation about his search he was asked whether he had ever been to Argentina. He had not but the question inspired him to travel there.

Upon arrival in Buenos Aires, Staton was impressed by the sophistication of the city. What most caught his attention, though, was the scant development of the local retail industry, especially given the size of the market in 1986 with a national population of thirty million. Shopping malls and food chains practically did not exist. What he saw led him to mentally sketch out an enormous business opportunity. He had been accustomed to staying afloat in competitive markets and felt that he had found the right place at the right time to open a McDonald's franchise. Just as was the case with Howard Head, Staton's unsatisfied personal need for growth led him to doggedly pursue this opportunity.

Staton opened his first Arcos Dorados ("golden arches") restaurant in the Belgrano district of Buenos Aires on November 22, 1986. Encouraged by his initial experience, he set a goal of opening an additional six to ten restaurants the following year. Staton had been drawn by the panorama of opportunities offered by Argentina's new democracy, educated citizens, and abundant natural resources. Unfortunately, emerging economies are much more unpredictable than those of the developed world. In 1987, the Argentinean economy began to stumble and, by 1989, it was firmly entangled in two processes of hyperinflation. The Arcos Dorados business had grown much more slowly than expected, with Staton only having been able to open four restaurants. Perhaps this was a good thing, though, as revenues during this period were insufficient to cover costs.

The sociopolitical situation in Argentina during the late 1980s was very tense. By pursuing criminal charges against and publicly criticizing the former military government, the newly elected democratic government enraged factions within the armed forces, which often threatened and occasionally rose up in protest. At the same time, the government had very little influence over the unions, whose frequent strikes kept the entire economy on the brink of collapse. The size of the state was excessively large and highly inefficient. As a result, the country had stagnated, and the fiscal deficit was beyond control. These circumstances exceeded the managerial capacity of the Raúl Alfonsín government. To cover the fiscal deficit, it resorted to expansion of the money supply. This resulted in price increases, prompting the public to buy more before additional rises and thereby further accelerating inflation. In these circumstances of economic stagnation, any increase in the money supply was passed on directly to prices. In short, the economy was caught in a deadly trap.

Staton decided to remain in business in Argentina and to use his personal savings to finance the deficits generated by Arcos Dorados. "Countries don't disappear," he observed. "I knew the situation would pass." In fact, once the turbulent period of hyperinflation was over, the economy did begin to stabilize and, from 1991, entered a period of strong growth. A wave of modernization during these years created an economic context especially favorable to innovation in the food industry. Arcos Dorados entered the market as an aspirational brand for the Argentinean middle and upper-middle classes—a marked difference in market, when compared with the McDonald's chain in the United States—and demand increased exponentially.

Staton finally had time to focus on business fundamentals. Gone was the need to adjust prices on an almost daily basis, or to pore over the paper every morning in search of any sign of economic recovery. Over the following years, the company's growth accelerated. By 1992, it owned ten restaurants in Buenos Aires; by 1993, that figure had risen to seventeen. By the middle of the decade, Arcos Dorados restaurants were spread across Argentina.

As a result of the company's high rate of growth, extensive organizational changes were required, and Staton invested all his energy in seeing them through. In this regard, his attitude was different from that of Howard Head, who opted to leave the businesses he had led as they adapted to new contexts. For Staton, though, organization was what he liked best about business. His challenge was to identify an alternative to the functional business structure that had seen Arcos Dorados through its early years.

A common tendency, when many companies seek to mitigate the challenges of growth, is to organize themselves based on a regional structure. Sometimes support functions, like finance or facilities or IT, provide services to all of the regions and are centralized at the corporate level. The company decided to manage its growth in Argentina by dividing the business based on four geographic zones. At first, this appeared to be a reasonable solution. Each zone had the same business functions as the others, although some continued to be exercised and implemented centrally at headquarters. This arrangement allowed for focus, facilitating active supervision by the director of each regional zone with respect to the most delicate processes of the business. To the extent the business continued to grow, moreover, the company could further divide its organization into additional subzones.

Emerging economies, however, are always a source of surprise, not all of which is agreeable. Macroeconomic activity in Argentina, which had been vigorous for several years, began to cool drastically in 1998. What started as a recession turned into a total collapse by the end of 2001. During the first quarter of 2002, the GDP contracted by 20 percent, with the overall annual contraction standing at about 11 percent by year's end. How was it possible that what had seemed an exemplary model for emerging economies in the mid-1990s could have fallen so low?

The economic reforms of the 1990s and their effects have a murky legacy that will continue to be the subject of evaluation and controversy well into the future. But in connection with the practical effects on Staton's business, it is sufficient to say that Argentina's fiscal deficit had continued to grow with no solution in sight. Although private investment in infrastructure had improved indicators measuring national productivity and had brought strong economic growth, mismanagement of public funds contributed to a marked increase in Argentina's external debt. This situation only further aggravated Argentina's problems in connection with its primary fiscal deficit. In 1999, Argentina elected a weak coalition government that, ultimately, was incapable of defusing the situation. Instead, strong depressions in international prices for agricultural commodities exacerbated it further. As a result, Argentina experienced institutional failure across the government in December 2001. Within the course of one week, the country had five presidents and the streets hummed with the rage of social unrest.

In one conversations reflecting on that time, Staton mentioned to Roberto the tremendously negative impact of regionalizing the company just as Argentina raced headlong into macroeconomic depression. The problem was simple. Although a regional structure allowed Arcos Dorados to benefit from an increased focus on business processes, it was expensive because, among other reasons, it required an executive-level manager in each of the four regions. The crisis obliged the company to partially reverse that decision and regroup into two subregions. Nonetheless, the decision to divide into the four geographic zones led to profound organizational learning, informing how it expanded into international markets at a later date. But that's another story.

THE NUMBERS BEHIND RECESSIONS

Just like taxes and death, recessions are unavoidable certainties. National economies oscillate between expansion stages—which are the most prevalent in the business cycle—and recessions or macroeconomic contractions, which are shorter in duration than expansionary stages but have dramatic consequences that last into even periods of expansion. Fortunately, due to their shorter duration, recessions are a sort of detour along the long-term growth trajectories of national economies. Their limited duration, however, does not make them feel any less painful when they materialize.

Although they are difficult to predict, recessions tend to be transitory phenomena that exhibit common patterns by which they can be identified, making them subject to analysis and study, thereby enabling managers to design and implement a response. Because they may be observed, businesses can take action to prepare for these economic certainties even if they seem a long way off. This is regardless of the fact that all recessions are different from one another. Indeed, recessions can be grouped into three broad categories based on the potential effects of the external environment on the organization. These three types are *minor recessions*, *major recessions*, and *sudden-stop, phoenix-miracle recessions*.

Minor recessions are more frequent in developed countries. A stable institutional framework helps to diminish—without offering a total cure—microeconomic volatility. As we have seen, between 1945 and 2019, there were eleven recessions in the United States, all of which, with the exception of the one experienced in 2007–9, can be described as minor. Nonetheless, even minor recessions have resulted in significant changes in the competitive pressures facing businesses and have catalyzed almost constant changes in the market shares that companies hold.

Stijn Claessens, Ayhan Kose, and Marco Terrones have conducted extensive research and comprehensive analyses of the frequency and duration of recessions across the globe between the years 1960 and 2007, right before the last great recession.[6] Their findings are summarized in the table.

As table 6.1 indicates, a typical OECD (Organization for Economic Cooperation and Development) country experienced about six recessions between 1960 and 2007. The typical recession lasts almost four quarters. This study also assesses that an average recession is associated with an output drop of roughly 2 percent (data not included in the table). Although recessions have become shorter and milder over time, they remain highly synchronized across countries.

TABLE 6.1. Recessions' frequency and duration between 1960 and 2007

OECD Country	Amount of Recessions	Length in Quarters	Drop in GDP	Time in Recession
Canada	3	4.00	-6.45%	6%
France	4	3.50	-2.57%	7%
Germany	8	3.25	-2.56%	13%
Italy	9	3.11	-2.67%	15%
Japan	3	4.67	-7.39%	7%
Great Britain	5	4.20	-8.44%	11%
United States	7	3.43	-3.16%	12%
Australia	7	3.43	-3.50%	12%
Austria	6	2.50	-1.60%	8%
Belgium	7	2.86	-1.53%	10%
Denmark	7	4.14	-4.11%	15%
Finland	5	4.60	-22.51%	12%
Greece	8	3.50	-11.83%	15%
Ireland	3	2.67	-1.41%	4%
The Netherlands	5	4.00	-0.82%	10%
New Zealand	12	3.83	-14.74%	24%
Norway	3	2.67	-2.99%	4%
Portugal	4	4.50	-6.68%	9%
Spain	4	3.00	-2.76%	6%
Sweden	3	7.33	-15.17%	11%
Switzerland	9	3.56	-6.86%	17%

The length of time during which certain countries were in recession in this period, defined as the fraction of quarters the economy is in recession over the full sample period, is truly surprising. For instance, New Zealand was in recession 24 percent of the time, Switzerland 17 percent, and both Denmark and Italy 15 percent. Some countries' GDPs experienced brutal cumulative collapses during their recessions. As an example, Finland experienced, on average, nearly a 22 percent drop in the size of its GDP. Despite their apparent magnitude, none of these examples represent major recessions.

A well-known example of a *major recession* is the Great Depression, which commenced with the collapse of the New York Stock Exchange on October 29, 1929. The world did not completely escape from this crisis until it was entrenched in World War II. More recently, the global crisis experienced between 2007 and 2009, even a decade later, continues to affect both businesses and national economies. In 2009, the GDP of the developed world contracted nearly 3.5 percent. Italy's output shrank by 3.5 percent, Germany's by 5.7 percent, and that of the United States by 2.6 percent.

The third type of recession is typically only seen in the emerging world. Given the relatively high degree of institutional weakness, macroeconomic volatility is more dramatic in these countries. While it is true that emerging economies also suffer minor recessions similar to those described above, they also suffer severe contractions that can be distinguished from major recessions because they are recovered from much more quickly. For instance, Argentina's economic crisis of 2002 entailed a contraction in the country's GDP of 11 percent, but by the next year it was growing quickly, demonstrating a "miraculous" recovery. For this reason, these types of events are described in terms of a *"sudden-stop"* followed by a *"phoenix miracle."*

In a study of thirty-one emerging economies between 1980 and 2004, Guillermo Calvo, Alejandro Izquierdo, and Ernesto Talvi identified thirty-four recessions.[7] The authors determined that roughly two-thirds of the recessions experienced in these economies could be described as sudden-stop, phoenix miracles, which, on average, implied negative growth of 7.8 percent of GDP, followed by a complete recovery within three years.

TABLE 6.2. Recessions' magnitude of contraction and time to full recovery

Country	GDP Peak Pre-Crisis	Year of Crisis	Magnitude of Contraction	Year of Recovery
Indonesia	1997	1998	-13%	2003
Malaysia	1997	1998	-7%	2000
Mexico	1994	1995	-6%	1997
Russia	1997	1998	-5%	1999
South Korea	1997	1998	-7%	1999
Thailand	1996	1998	-12%	2002
Turkey 1	1993	1994	-5%	1995
Turkey 2	1998	1999	-3%	2000

Table 6.2 presents a summary of data gathered in connection with recessions in emerging economies.[8]

We can observe a clear difference between the developing world with respect to the magnitude of recessions. According to the work of Calvo and his colleagues, these recoveries have a special dynamic. They occur in the context of a virtual disappearance of access to debt markets and are strongly leveraged by salary reductions in order to finance the recovery of businesses.

In summary, executives worldwide face principally three types of economic recessions: minor and short, major and long, and major and short. Although it is true that some recessions are considered moderate, they are always challenging phenomena that shrink demand, affect credit, and leave millions of people unemployed. How can this be positive for an organization? What does this mean for business strategy and what are the principal leadership stresses generated by recessions? We will address these questions in the following pages.

WAS SCHUMPETER WRONG?

With Arcos Dorados, Wood Staton pushed an agenda of creative destruction, introducing radical innovation into the Argentinean food industry.

During the early years, though, it would appear that the Schumpeterian process was less important than macroeconomic instability. To elaborate: in the first half of the twentieth century, the economist Joseph Schumpeter argued that capitalism entailed an ongoing cycle of innovation and creative destruction. This can be understood in terms of a sequence that commences with a radical innovation that transforms traditional ways of doing business but is then followed by imitation, which has the effect of eroding the gains of innovation until the next business shift begins. Schumpeter's understanding of industrial evolution, for our purposes, is helpful in addressing strategic leadership challenges, enabling us to identify strategic priorities and to anticipate systemic losses. The question remains, however, concerning whether Schumpeter's ideas apply in countries that experience macroeconomic turbulence.

Staton's experience would suggest that they do, as evidenced by his belief that there were far fewer business opportunities in Argentina in the 2010s than there had been during the economic turbulence of the late 1980s. The industry dynamic, as described by Schumpeter, was dominant over the macroeconomic processes. If you possess an entrepreneurial mindset, then macroeconomic instability is just another contingency to manage while you seek out and act on those opportunities.

One of the risks of operation during turbulent periods is that it is easy to lose touch or to underestimate the central forces that drive business. Organizational development is informed and shaped by the need to satisfy market demands in creative ways. The macroeconomic context affects only temporarily the internal dynamics of an industry. Nonetheless, even though industry dynamics are the dominant force, temporary changes in the economic context may give rise to permanent changes in the competitive position of a business, and this is a critical aspect to remember. The Schumpeterian process dominates, but the contingent effect of a recession might permanently alter the market equilibrium and a company's competitive position.

In this respect, a fundamental skill is to understand how the macroeconomic context will affect the development of the general business model that predominates in the industry. To do this, a manager must have identified the developmental stage in which the industry currently finds itself and the competitive position of the organization within the industry at a particular time and place. Recessions open opportunities to dramatically change a company's competitive position. This happens as a result of the company's current position, not in spite of it. Senior management teams have the opportunity to obtain a competitive jump that strengthens their companies' positions—the chance for a competitive leapfrog. For that, they need to clearly understand how a recession can affect their company and understand their rivals' competitive advantages.[9]

When a company adopts a competitive position within an industry, it creates competitive defenses. As we have discussed already, these defenses are based on factors centered on the consumer value proposition and other factors relating to production. There are many barriers to overcome in order to defend a position. A defensive mechanism based on the consumer is, for example, a type of objective or subjective differentiation. The relationship between consumers and leading brands is partially based on these differentiating attributes. We may prefer Coca-Cola or Pepsi over generic supermarket brands because we prefer their flavor, but this preference may also be based on the brand meaning something to our individual identities. Similarly, we might prefer an iPhone to other smartphones not only because of the intrinsic characteristics of the product but also because of the need to belong to a social group. Nonetheless, the status quo of brand identification may be more likely to be challenged and change during a recession. People whose family income has been reduced may choose to purchase a generic brand rather than go without. Recessions lower the relative value of differentiating attributes and encourage consumers who are suffering economically to try new brands.

Roberto and his colleagues analyzed firms' market share evolution across 64 US industries between 1982 and 2015. Their study included three US recessions. The authors explored the effect of different sources of competitive advantages on market share evolution during and in the aftermath of these recessions. They observed that advertisement and R&D expenditure negatively correlated with market share while cost-related expenses had a positive correlation. They also observed a positive relationship between the degree of firm-level financial flexibility and the increase in market share during and after the recessions.[10]

How, though, does an organization convert short-term trends into a permanent change to its competitive position? In most cases, and especially in connection with relatively short-lived recessions that fail to permanently alter the consumer's purchasing habits, these will revert to normal when the economy recovers. What is it that organizations need to do to turn a transitory phenomenon into an ongoing advantage?

HYUNDAI AGAINST THE WORLD

The Hyundai story provides a good example of a competitive move that makes the most of a recession. The company entered the US market in 1985 and, just like every other late entrant into a mature market, it was required to occupy a niche with a very well-defined competitive position based on differentiation from the major players. Hyundai chose to position itself as an economical brand; however, its vehicles proved to be unreliable. Its first car, the Excel, quickly gained a reputation for its poor-quality car, giving the company a reputation, whether justified or not, that endured for more than a decade.

In the early 1990s, Hyundai began a process of change, starting with a quality improvement program. Such was the effect that, by 1994, Hyundai had moved from nineteenth position to eleventh on a US national survey of automotive dealer satisfaction with manufacturers. In 1998, the company doubled down on this bet, introducing a manufacturer's warranty that lasted for either ten years or 100,000 miles of travel, whichever came first. This was a way of signaling to the market how the company had changed in terms of the reliability and quality of its products.

Unfortunately, for Hyundai, potential customers were not convinced. The cost of trying out a Hyundai—a durable good that is purchased with scant frequency—was too high. It did not matter what reports said about the quality of the vehicles when people were concerned that they could lose thousands of dollars, as well as valuable time, if they found, post-purchase, that the cars did not live up to the hype. Consequently, despite its guarantee program, the investment in quality, and favorable reports from industry specialists, Hyundai barely reached 1 percent of market share by 1999. Industry maturity gives market positions a certain rigidity. Gaining market share in these conditions is practically impossible, unless the company buys one of its competitor organizations. Nonetheless, by 2011, Hyundai's market share had risen to 5.1 percent. So, what happened during the intervening years?

Hyundai's drastic repositioning within the market cannot be understood without accounting for the effect of recessions in competitive processes. While Hyundai battled for greater market share in the US automotive industry throughout the 1990s, tech companies grew at a high rate based on the promise of exceptional future returns. These organizations attracted huge investments from the capital markets. However, as the dot.com companies responsible for the stock market boom failed to deliver the expected returns, investors lost faith and sold their shares, driving a slump that triggered the 2001 recession.

By the time of the recession, Hyundai had achieved a 2 percent market share. It had taken fifteen years and significant expenditure to secure a 1 percent share and only two more years and much less investment to double it. In a sense, the recession helped Hyundai to capitalize on its quality control efforts of the previous years. Many customers could no longer delay the purchase of a new family vehicle, but the recession had severely constrained their family budgets. People previously reticent about committing to the Hyundai brand now decided to give it a try. They discovered their expectations regarding quality were wrong, and that Hyundai cars offered much more than they had anticipated.

Once the market crawled out of recession, Hyundai again had to compete for market share, gaining only another 1 percent between 2002 and 2008, at the cost of millions of dollars promoting the brand. Then history repeated itself, with the recession of 2007–9 coinciding with the company's leap to a 5 percent market share. All of which begs the question: will we have to wait for another recession for consumers to be once again receptive to Hyundai's message about product quality? Maybe so, unless industry innovation shakes up the market and initiates a new Schumpeterian cycle.

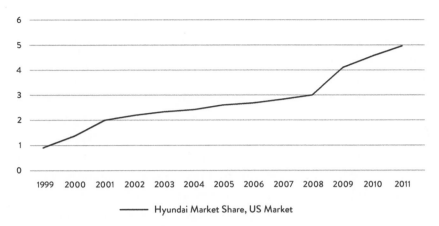

FIGURE 6.1. Hyundai's market share evolution.
Source: KNOEMA.

The auto industry, for example, appears to be entering such a cycle right now with the rise of the electric car, autonomous vehicles, and the innovations of Tesla, among others.[11]

THE INTERPLAY BETWEEN COMPETITIVE STRATEGY AND FINANCIAL FLEXIBILITY

Carlos Slim is a Mexican businessman who became one of the richest people in the world. His personal wealth and success in business are founded on taking advantage of a cycle of regular recessions and subsequent recoveries. Like George Soros and Warren Buffett, Slim seems to follow the example of Baron Rothschild who ghoulishly recommended the purchase of assets when there is blood in the streets. For example, Slim acted on opportunities in the wake of the "tequila crash," following the devaluation of the Mexican peso against the US dollar at the end of 1994, substantially adding to his fortune.

During recessions, increases in unemployment create personal financial difficulties for consumers, which has a knock-on effect on businesses and banks.[12] A bank's fear of not receiving payment leads it to limit lending activities in an effort to improve the quality of its portfolio. This reaction aggravates the employment situation and shifts part of the problems associated with the risk of default to the rest of the business world, which finally discovers that it may not have credit just when it is most needed. This is bad news for businesses that heed the siren call of bank representatives offering "soft" credit in times of bonanza. Solvent companies, however, find themselves with much greater strategic liberty during recessions. The flexibility afforded by a less leveraged financial structure leaves companies in an optimal position to develop long-term competitive advantages.

The empirical evidence at the research level supports this anecdotal evidence. For instance, Roberto and his colleagues analyzed the effect of financial flexibility on M&A (mergers and acquisitions) activity during and after US recessions. They observed a strong and significantly positive effect: companies with the highest financial flexibility had the highest amount of M&A activity. As financial flexibility decreases—with the ratios of debt to assets increasing—the M&A activity significantly reduces. Overall, this study found that financial flexibility acts as a strong predictor of M&A activity. Managers need to take the cost of flexibility in consideration—that is, the opportunity cost of financial assets without specific investments.

The case of Martifer is an extreme example of not adequately considering the value of financial flexibility. Founded by two brothers, Carlos Martins and Jorge Martins, the Portuguese company Martifer was the leader in the 1990s of Europe's metal structure industry, with a high market share on the Iberian Peninsula and a significant presence across Europe. By the turn of the century, the company had developed strong competitive advantages by creating barriers to entry into its market. But the Martins brothers aspired to more that the metal structure industry could not satisfy. Pushed by its determined leadership, Martifer entered into various other industries, including renewable energy systems, electrical generation, agriculture, and biofuels.

As a result of the velocity of the company's growth and its commitment to its employees, the Martins brothers were named businessmen of the year in Portugal. But the firm's rapid growth was financed by credit. By the time of the economic recession of 2007–9, the company was burdened with debt.[13] Martifer had to undertake strict cost reductions and sell a range of its assets, resulting in significant financial losses and an extraordinary level of organizational pain. This is the flipside of Slim's success story. The most interesting aspect of the changes both experienced is that neither the gains nor losses were necessarily related to good or bad product-related competitive strategies. Rather, asset management was the key activity to each company's repositioning within their market's competitive framework.

THE PROS AND CONS OF FINANCIAL FLEXIBILITY

Financial flexibility is simply a tool to achieve managerial maneuverability during recessions, and it can come with significant competitive costs—the cost of not investing. Harvard professor Pankaj Ghemawat broadly studies the pros and cons of strategic flexibility in different contexts. During recessions, he encourages managers to pay attention simultaneously to financial and competitive risks. The risk of investment can be outweighed by the competitive risk of not investing and, as a result, losing long-term market share.[14] Competitive strategies interact with liquidity positions and macroeconomic restrictions and, together, may result in significant gains or losses for companies and their investors.

As this book went to print, Roberto and his colleagues were examining this trade-off in a research study centered on those US industries most affected by recessions in the three decades preceding the coronavirus pandemic.[15] The study seeks to evaluate the effect of different levels of operating leverage and financial flexibility on performance. Operating leverage is the ratio of fixed-to-variable costs. Companies create cost advantages by increasing the operating leverage, as investing in large and modern facilities improves scale economies, operating efficiency, and market power. Consequently, they can significantly strengthen their competitive positions during and after recessions. However, increasing the operating leverage reduces the degree of financial flexibility. In Ghemawat's terms, as the competitive risk of not investing decreases, the financial risk rises owing to increased financial investments.[16]

Overperformers were those that master the combination of financial and competitive risks. However, they also excel in M&A activity during recessions. When they invest, they decide between expanding their plant capacity or acquiring the assets of competitors in financial distress. Successful navigation of recessions and business cycles is a matter of a complex combination of these elements. We want to close the chapter with more general recommendations and, in the next chapter, shed light on the leadership dilemmas that emerge when setting strategic priorities for dealing with recessions.

THE STRATEGIC FRAMEWORK BEHIND
MASTERING THE EMERGENCY CHALLENGE

What are the most noteworthy characteristics of the strategic moves in the above examples? What are the practical implications of the ongoing research on recessions? In order to organize and make more accessible the principal lessons of these strategic maneuvers, we categorize business decisions based on four criteria: demand-based competitive isolating mechanisms, supply-based competitive isolating mechanisms, innovation, and strategic flexibility. Any strategy that does not account for and harmonically integrate the company's position with respect to these four elements is not likely to survive a recession. The first two characteristics explain the sources and stability of your company's competitive positioning. This is informed by the isolating mechanisms that are in place as they serve as barriers that decrease competitive pressures. They may be demand-centered, or they may be related to the organization's operations.

Companies with high levels of differentiation are those that base their business strategies on isolating mechanisms that are dependent on demand. In Apple's case, for example, there is a focus on understanding demand, establishing a sense of community, developing an attractive interface, and creating unique designs. The principal weakness of businesses that leverage demand-based mechanisms is that in times of economic crisis, their relative value is diminished unless they are in the luxury segment of the market.

Cost-based competitors build their competitive position on supply-based isolating mechanisms. Android's original isolation mechanisms were cost-based. Its value proposition emphasizes the open structure of its community, in which users collaborate to contribute more value to the community. Although Samsung uses the Android operating system and positions its smartphones close to Apple products, overall, Android-based products were often less expensive than Apple products. The Spanish retailer Mercadona bases its business strategy on isolation mechanisms related to supply, as they combine well with business models oriented toward cost advantages. Mercadona does not waste funds on publicity and focuses instead on creating products that feature its own brand name.

The positive aspects of cost-based strategies increase during recessions. While they are always useful, they are especially useful during economic contractions. The challenge here is to persuade the customer to remain loyal to a cost leader once the economy begins to grow again and the relative value of differentiating attributes increases. This would confound a familiar pattern whereby, in practice, many companies emerge or grow during economic recessions and then contract once the recovery is on its way.

The third element of this model is innovation, regardless of whether it is radical or incremental. Generally, innovation is the best strategy with which to confront a macroeconomic contraction. Danone's strategy during the Argentinean recession of 2002 is illustrative of this point. From 2002 onward, Danone grew its market share by aggressively undertaking new product launches that increased per capita spending on fresh dairy products in Argentina. Similarly, the acceleration of e-commerce worldwide during years of recession is another example of how—by way of innovation—companies can grow and reach a sustainable position.

Strategic flexibility is the final element of the strategic framework for mastering recession. Winning market share without significant commercial effort is possible for companies that maintain financial liquidity over long periods. For example, instead of falling into the temptation to increase debt in order to earn greater amounts in times of bonanza, these companies follow a more conservative path. The reader should note, though, that financial flexibility is only one aspect of strategic flexibility. Another is the active management of the product portfolio. For instance, many consumer products companies launch their low-cost brands during recessions. When the economy recovers, these companies stop offering those brands.

Strategic flexibility is not only subject to a company's internal decision-making but also is influenced by external factors. One facet of strategic flexibility involves limitations created by the strengths and strategic maneuvers of competitors. In 2002, Danone's Argentinean competitors in the dairy product market were experiencing difficulties, whether as a result of global issues, as was the case with Parmalat, or as the result of local issues that affected companies like Sancor. The relative weakness of its competitors amplified Danone's strategic flexibility in the years immediately following the crisis. But the situation was different when Danone had to face the global recession of 2007–9 and its competitors were in a much stronger financial position.

Another aspect of strategic flexibility that is not subject to a firm's control are governmental decisions taken during a crisis. During the 2007–9 crisis, for example, the US government offered financial support to the big three of the Detroit automotive world. This action reduced the levels of strategic flexibility available to Hyundai to capitalize and profit from its quality improvement program.

FINAL REMARKS

These examples sketch out a simple analytical framework for designing an organization's business strategy in a manner that takes into consideration business cycles, recessions, and recoveries. The four pillars of the framework, when viewed only descriptively, hide powerful and dynamic causation mechanisms that affect how the model functions. Recessions should be conceived of as a scale that tips in favor of cost-based competitive advantages during a limited number of quarters only to swing back in favor of differentiation-based advantages following recovery. Strategic flexibility is like a master key that fortifies a company's capacity to take advantage of the shifts in the relative value of the different types of competitive isolation mechanisms. Innovation acts to mitigate or moderate the negative effects caused by the trade-off between cost-based and demand-based isolation mechanisms and their relative changes in value. It diminishes the need for the broadest strategic flexibility by affording companies the ability to alter their product offering or operations in response to relative changes in value between competitive isolation mechanisms.

This framework is simple, but mastering its use requires managerial capacity of the highest levels of strategic sophistication. We have yet to discuss the significant leadership tensions to which these aspects of a company's strategic operations will give rise. This is a matter to which we will now turn.

CHAPTER 7

NAVIGATING
THE EMERGENCY
CHALLENGE

The exercise of leadership in times of recession demands a rare combination of strategic foresight and management skills. To this end, in the previous chapter we examined the salient regularities of the macroeconomic context evolution. We aimed to provide order and structure to the evolution of an environment (the overall economy) that often appears mysterious or dark. Managers who assess macroeconomic evolutionary patterns are prepared to take advantage of recessions, ready to mobilize their companies. This chapter will explore how this can be done.

WHAT DOES LEAPFROGGING MEAN FOR YOUR COMPANY?

In order to effectively navigate the next recession, senior management teams will need to define the type of competitive leapfrogging strategy that their companies may profit from. Leapfrogging relates to improvement changes in the current strategic positioning. At a general level, companies could follow a differentiated or a cost strategy and do that as a market leader or as a niche player. Depending on the strategy, companies have alternative types of leapfrogging opportunities, which, in turn, will determine the set of strategic priorities and, consequently, the type of losses that different organizational factions will face.

For differentiated leaders like Danone, leapfrogging means increasing long-term market share and, in the long term, enhancing brand equity. In fact, during periods of emergency, differentiators have to be prepared to grow their investment in brand equity.

To increase market share, the likelihood of competitive leapfrogging for differentiated companies has different alternatives. A quick win emerges in line with the opportunity to increase per-capita consumption through innovation. If products have not yet reached market saturation, it might be beneficial to accelerate penetration during recessions instead of re-trenching. Furthermore, differentiators should address product afford-ability, avoiding price increases wherever possible. Their focus should be on products and services that have a better fit with recessionary markets. This does not mean lowering prices but making them more affordable, reducing consumer products' size or volume. Additionally, companies can practice adaptive pricing, capitalizing on the fact that different customers have different needs.[1]

If the industry is already mature, though, and market growth prospects are low, only an effective trade-off between operating and financial flexibility will make it possible to leapfrog competitors. As the impact of a recession increases, with demand declining sharply, there is a higher likelihood that competitors with high operational costs may exit the industry. It is financial flexibility and liquidity that can ensure a company's survival.

It is imperative, therefore, that they monitor their competitors' situation for signs of financial strength or weakness, making reasonable adjustments in their organization. In particular, leaders may want to consider asset re-configuration opportunities to improve operation and performance, making acquisitions, alliances, internal developments, and divestments as required.

For cost leaders, the fundamental challenge is to persuade customers to remain loyal once the economy begins to recover, consumers have more dis-posable income, and the relative value of product differentiation increases. Many companies that occupy low-cost niches either are founded or grow during recessions, but they subsequently experience difficulties that force some of them out of business when the economy bounces back.

If your company is in a similar position to that of Hyundai during the 1990s, you will need to prepare to reposition it in order to leapfrog competitors. Hyundai had to shift from being a cost-oriented company to a high-quality one, improving consumers' willingness to pay in the process. Whereas cost leaders may be sure to benefit from consumers' product substitution during the next recession, their challenge is to turn this transitory shift into a permanent consumer choice. In so doing, aggressive investment in product quality is a must. This strategy has worked particularly well in mature industries.

Mastering recessions requires sophisticated managerial foresight. Nonetheless, to fully take advantage of the opportunities that can result from recessions, managers need to distinguish between leadership challenges when recessions look far in the horizon from managing recessions periods.

LEADERSHIP CHALLENGES WHEN RECESSIONS SEEM FAR AWAY

The emergency challenge relates to a company's navigation of a recession. However, leadership challenges start long before then, during periods of economic growth. It is necessary to build recession resistance within organizations, especially those that wish to make a healthy increase in their market share during the next recession. As we have demonstrated, preparing your company for recessions requires the development of strategic flexibility. The problem is that flexibility is rarely achieved for free; it carries a cost that manifests itself in different forms and can have a visible impact on the short-term profit and losses statement.

A company could decide to increase strategic flexibility by decreasing financial and operating leverage levels. This is likely to create tension for some factions within the organization. How best to decrease financial leverage? One possibility is to reduce the amount of customer lending or become stricter in credit ratings with a view to improving liquidity. Such a move, though, will upset the sales department. Another option is to reduce investments in manufacturing thereby decreasing the level of operational leverage. There is likely to be resistance from the manufacturing department, which would suffer in terms of efficiency.

Alternatively, businesses could diversify their product portfolios. This would seek to maintain brand equity through the availability of more affordable products during the downturn in demand. However, this path would entail the sacrifice of unit margins. Its impact on performance incentives inevitably would lead to resistance within the sales department. Overall, the set of priorities necessary to navigate recessionary contexts results in a set of losses that are unevenly distributed across the organization, highlighting the need for leaders to thoroughly understand and address organizational losses.

PREDICTING THE NEXT RECESSION

Senior managers have to scan constantly for external clues in order to detect the likelihood of a recession occurring. They can undertake some of this work themselves and, where budgets allow, hire experts to share their economic forecasts with the management team. As we have already suggested, economies enter into recession with some regularity, so tracking the passage of time since the last one is an essential method for anticipating when the next is likely to begin. In the United States, on average, the economy contracts every decade. So, if five years have passed since the end of the last recession, now would be a good time to start thinking about how you will weather the next one.

The inversion of Treasury bond yield curves is a strong indicator of an imminent recession, possibly within the next twelve to eighteen months. In a normal yield curve, the short-term bills yield less than the long-term bonds. During economic booms, the yield on a thirty-year bond will be approximately three points higher than the yield on a three-month bill in the United States. Investors tend to expect lower returns when their money is tied up for a shorter period, and, in turn, expect higher profits from a long-term investment. When investors have little confidence in the economy in the short term, the yield curve inverts. Investors will then demand higher returns for short-term investments, in comparison with long-term investments, as they perceive the former to be riskier. This is a clear sign that a recession is around the corner.

Notwithstanding the tools employed to assess the likelihood of recessions, it is important to remember that the purpose of this exercise is to introduce "hard facts" that help to raise awareness among organizational leaders of the proximity of an economic downturn. The top management team bears the ultimate responsibility for acting on the intelligence in its possession and leading the organization successfully through the downturn. It is essential, therefore, that external warning and forecasting mechanisms are in place, informed by systemic observation of the overall economy, your industry structure and performance, your competitors, and your own organization.

THE HIDDEN SYSTEMIC TENSIONS WHEN PREPARING TO HIT A RECESSION

Systemic observation allows managers to generate conjectures about the potential resistance from organizational factions that they may face when attempting to implement strategies to prepare for recessions. Failure to do so may lead to inadequate diagnosis and cripple an organization's ability to move in the right direction.

Consider a scenario where a recession has not yet hit, but the senior management team estimates that the odds that it will occur within the next twelve to eighteen months are high. If management acts quickly, it may both mitigate potential losses and strengthen the company's strategic positioning. For that, it is essential to mobilize the organization to take advantage of these possibilities, maintaining it in a state of readiness, and avoiding the trap of task evasion. What is out of sight should not remain out of mind. There is always a danger, otherwise, that organizational leadership will underestimate the likelihood of a near-term recession and the adverse effects and losses it may create.

Senior managers need to pay particular attention to what happens during strategic planning meetings. What behaviors do you observe in the managers involved? What kind of tensions emerge? Are there specific initiatives that are resisted more than expected? Who is trying to lead the discussion about the challenge ahead and who is trying to avoid it? Leaders should be mindful of falling into cognitive traps, establishing shared understanding of the threats and opportunities in a recession, and recognizing where resistance has its roots in a given faction's fears about the losses they will incur. In short, systemic observation requires the close monitoring of meeting dynamics and an understanding of the agendas that inform the arguments, advocacy, and decisions of representatives from different groups within the organization.

TYPICAL SOURCES OF CONFLICT DURING THE EMERGENCY CHALLENGE

While there may be myriad sources of potential conflict, our research suggests that in order to navigate recessions successfully, senior management teams will need to orchestrate two main conflicts that typically emerge at the organizational level. The first pertains to financial flexibility. Reducing financial leverage typically requires that several projects will need to be postponed. The owners of these projects are expected to offer resistance as they are likely to perceive this situation as a loss.

The second is concerned with the trade-off between unit margins and market share. In order to leapfrog competitors and gain a sustainable share of the market, it is often necessary to temporarily reduce unit margins during times of recession. On their part, shareholders may put pressure on the management team to protect margins until the downturn is over. As these tensions are likely to emerge when preparing the company for recession, leaders need to have clarity of understanding, avoiding simplistic assumptions and finger pointing, such as arguing that stakeholders lack any sense of urgency. Leaders need to assess and map out where losses are likely to occur and which factions will be affected. Without such insight, their strategies for dealing with the recession are likely to fail.

EXERCISING LEADERSHIP DURING TIMES OF TROUBLE

No matter how much time and energy are invested in preparation for the regular cycles of economic contraction, few situations are more dramatic than when a country slides into a general recession. Emotionally, the situation is different from the occasions when a business is involved in a specific competitive challenge. When an industry progresses from the development stage to maturity, internal tensions within organizations in that industry will arise. However, a company's personnel know that the outcome is largely in their own hands and that, if they fail, they will have multiple opportunities to look for work elsewhere. In a general recession, however, things look very different and employees cannot feel confident about either of these factors. There is a widespread feeling, whether justified or not, that nothing can be done about the macroeconomic context. The cost of failure, moreover, is extraordinarily high. Increased rates of unemployment can last for months or even years, negatively impacting both personal well-being and the recovery of the national economy as a whole.

Leading in recessions means confronting the profound fear felt by the people in the organization. Management should conduct systemic analyses that endeavor to reach beyond the proper boundaries of the organization. Suppliers and business clients alike should be included in this diagnosis and, ideally, they should play a role in the corresponding adaptive intervention. When the problem experienced affects an entire country, the adaptive solution should reach beyond the organization at least into the directly proximate links in the value chain. For this reason, the term *systemic observation* should take on extremely broad dimensions during an emergency challenge.

Conflictual interpretation during emergency situations takes on a unique characteristic: losses are temporary, but their potential competitive impact can be long term. This requires a special mastery when assessing pain points within the organization. As you may have concluded while reading this chapter, a recession automatically shifts the gaze of all toward cost concerns. In practice, this implies an assortment of direct losses, however heterogeneously distributed they may be throughout the organization. From a leadership perspective, there is a serious risk in funneling losses toward the links that are the weakest in the chain. Generally, this will provoke painful learning experiences that will affect organization cohesion in the long term.

Adaptive intervention takes on a very particular form during emergency leadership challenges. When a company enters a severe recession with low levels of strategic flexibility, it is highly probable that it must embark on a broad cost-cutting exercise. This often means terminating the employment contracts of some personnel. The less strategic flexibility there is, the greater the urgency in directing this process. The temptation to move toward authoritarian behavior is strong, especially because of the strong deference often shown to formal authority in these situations. Any organizational learning process should address the following: adjustments that have to be made without compromising the organization's long-term competitive position; care for employees and their employment; and a review of past mistakes that made the company vulnerable to the adverse effects of a recession.

These areas of focus should be at the center of any discussion in an adaptive intervention process. As a result of the urgency of the circumstances, it may be tempting to place too much emphasis on the first question, to deal only in passing with the second, and to never take the third into consideration. It is vital, therefore, that the managers leading the adaptive learning process maintain enough tension and balance throughout the process, ensuring that there is sufficient depth and breadth to the search for and assessment of potential solutions. These managers need to prevent the organization from running too quickly toward solutions that may be effective in the short term but are damaging to the organization's long-term future.

Here we must highlight the very peculiar danger that an organization's conduct can transform a recession into an accelerator of far-reaching consequences that have arisen from previous organizational errors. If a business has suffered competitive deterioration as a result of a succession of misguided decisions, the recession can often magnify their effects. When this dynamic begins to unfold, there is a tendency toward avoidance behavior, such as blaming the recession for matters that are, in reality, the result of organizational incompetence. When this happens, intervention is often necessary from those without hierarchical authority or formal responsibilities in order to facilitate effective learning. It goes without saying that such intervention carries significant personal risk for those that undertake it. However, when well executed, it represents a unique opportunity to correct structural problems in an organization.

THE NEED TO CARE FOR THE HOLDING ENVIRONMENT DURING RECESSIONS

Creating a holding environment during emergency challenges is imperative, especially when considering the impact that recessions can have on alternative employment opportunities in the event of business failure. A holding environment can take on diverse forms in an adaptive intervention. Sometimes this is accomplished through extreme conduct, as exemplified by the management team of Cambre, a manufacturer of residential and industrial electrical equipment, during Argentina's deep crash in 2002. The company's owner brought all the personnel together and stated, "We have cash to last us 4 months; this is the time we have to find a solution to our current crisis situation. If we do well, we will all celebrate. And if we do poorly, we will all go home. Until that time, there will be no dismissals." Authentic messages like these can galvanize people to seek out creative solutions to the emergency challenge.

It is possible, however, that many firms are too weak during a recession to build the type of holding environment created by Cambre. If that is the case, then as soon as the emergency situation is over the first priority should be to start planning for how to deal with the next recession. Once the economy has recovered, those organizations that were caught out by the recession are likely to continue suffering losses, ceding ground to their competitors. The risk of losing market share during times of economic growth as a direct result of the impact of a recession should not be underestimated. This is why planning, preparation, and learning lessons from past errors are all essential. They place an organization in a better position to take advantage of opportunities when they arise as well as to recover quickly and effectively from each downturn in the economy.[2]

BRIEF GUIDE
to Spotting and Responding to Emergency Challenge

SCAN THE EXTERNAL ENVIRONMENT

**Figure Out What Is Happening in the Country and Generate
an Assessment of the Need for Strategic Flexibility**

When you scan the environment, you need to think at your country level, not at your industry level. The senior management team needs to assess the probability of entering into a recession shortly and determine the organization's level of strategic flexibility. You can make conjectures, counting the years from the last recession, or observing whether the treasury bond yield curves start to invert, or commissioning an in-depth macroeconomic study. If your company opts not to forecast when the next recession will hit, it will need to permanently increase the organization's level of strategic flexibility in a state of general readiness to adapt.

Understand the Effect of the Recession on Your Competitive Positioning

At this point, you have to shift the analysis from the country level to the industry or competitive level. Assess the central competitive positioning in your industry, your competitors' financial health, and the different pressures you and they will face during the recession. Discuss opportunities for leapfrogging as well as the likelihood of being leapfrogged.

SCAN THE INTERNAL ENVIRONMENT— MAKE INTERPRETATIONS—MOBILIZE

Distinguish between Pressures Generated by Management Errors and Those Created by the Recession

During a recession, the organization tends to blame all its ills on poor macroeconomic conditions. This can be a deadly trap since you might be glossing over managerial errors that are unrelated to the current recession. There is a risk, therefore, that leadership abdicates responsibility by apportioning blame elsewhere. In order to have useful conversations, your team needs to both self-assess and to monitor the actions and performance of your competitors. Facts and honesty can counter initial resistance and the impulse to moan rather than act.

Push Your Company to Think about Its Long-Term Strategic Positioning and the Road toward Achieving It

The worst strategic reaction during a recession is to focus only on the short-term revenue statement. Even though it is natural to want to firefight, you need to avoid rushing toward short-term solutions. Even during recessions, it is important to keep in mind your long-term strategic positioning, discussing what steps need to be taken to achieve it and what setbacks necessitate a change of approach or priorities.

Start Mobilizing the Organization to See Recessions as Unique Opportunities for Competitive Leapfrogging

The most significant pain lies in the absence of opportunities if the company's response fails. Build a broad holding environment that allows for cross-organizational thinking. Reflect on the past macroeconomic cycles while engaging in the process of strategic foresight. Identify trade-offs between long-term and short-term business strategies and emphasize opportunities for competitive leapfrogging.

CHAPTER 8

THE STRUCTURAL
CHALLENGE

The structural challenge relates to the leadership dilemmas and business opportunities confronting a senior management team of a commodity-based company when commodity prices decrease. If you manage a company based on commodities, this chapter is for you. If you do not belong to such an industry, you might be tempted to skip this chapter. However, we believe you will find material and insights here that are useful regardless of what industry you work in.

The products generated by the commodities industries, based as they are on natural resources, undergo little change. As such, many people find this sector unattractive, long-established as it is, lacking in novelty value. Of the ten most valuable companies in July 2021 in terms of market capitalization in the world, only one had an interest in natural resources: Saudi Aramco. Moreover, organizations in these industries tend to grow more slowly in comparison with those from other, vibrant sectors like technology.

However, natural resource industries are much more relevant for economic welfare than usually is assumed. Several developed countries like

Australia, Canada, and Sweden base their economic development on those industries, while reliance on them is even more notable for emerging economies. In terms of global trade, in some years, commodities can account for around one-third of the total value.

Critical to our argument in *Strategy as Leadership* is the fact that the competitive dynamics in natural resource industries differ significantly from that of other sectors. The evolution of competitive pressures and the determinants of success and growth are driven by forces that fundamentally diverge from those of industries with products that allow for a certain degree of differentiation.

In this chapter, we deal with a fundamental leadership challenge that competitors in the commodities industries usually face: recurrent price changes. Commodity prices follow regular oscillations of varying lengths. Those that endure for decades are known as *supercycles*, whereas those of shorter duration, lasting a few years or less, are known simply as *cycles*.[1]

The constant ups and downs entail recurrent changes of priority. The switch of strategic focus determines a different set of organizational losses that might resist new priorities. Yet, senior management teams need to shift priorities repeatedly, adapting to long-term trends and their anticipated effects. They have to accommodate and adjust to the oscillations of both cycles and supercycles. The goal of this chapter is to facilitate the sensemaking of cyclical price fluctuations and enhance the likelihood of successful strategy implementation.

While acknowledging that companies will face periods during which prices continue to rise, nevertheless, our primary focus here will be on those moments when prices drop, triggering the structural challenge.

THE UPS AND DOWNS OF AN ITALIAN IMMIGRANT FAMILY

Roberto's family's history has long been intertwined with natural-resource-based businesses and their evolution. At least as far back as the time of his great-great-grandfather, Rafael Vassolo, the history includes periods of booms, stagnation, slumps, and recovery that occurred alternately through times of joy followed by others of grief, with no apparent escape from the cycle.

Rafael was born in Pietrabondante, Italy, a town located deep within the Molise region. Fleeing poverty and hunger, he landed in the port of Buenos Aries in 1874. By the turn of the twentieth century, the family had amassed 12,000 head of cattle—an impressive number for a group of immigrants that had arrived penniless.

Years went by in which the family continued to amass wealth with almost monotonous regularity. Human history, though, rarely follows a linear, upward path. There are always detours and bumps in the road. While the Vassolo family's wealth could be measured in heads of cattle and sacks of grain far in excess of what they had imagined in their old homeland, they were not at ease. What was the cause of their concern? The land they worked did not belong to them but was leased from others.

Leasing land had gone well for them, but the family wondered whether it was time to convert some of their cattle into their own landholdings. At the root of this question lies a typical dilemma for natural-resource-based businesses: the tension between asset turnover and security. Retaining capital in the form of livestock and crops meant that the family's assets had higher turnover on rented lands than would be the case on land they owned themselves. Converting capital into land meant that fewer funds would be available to invest in income-producing assets, which in the short- to mid-term would result in a reduction in annual income.

In 1908, the family decided to sell all of their livestock, which then numbered 10,000 head of cattle and 22,500 sheep. With the funds, they purchase two properties, one measuring 1,880 hectares and another composed of 2,530 hectares. They had made their choice, opting for a more secure business, less exposed to risk but with a lower return on assets.

As it happened, in 1909-10 there was a major drought in the region, resulting in high animal mortality rates. Fortunately for the family, the decision to divest livestock and invest in land protected the family's fortune, to some extent. Had they kept the cattle and continued cultivating crops, as in the past, the fruits of much of their forty years of labor would have disappeared as a result of the drought.

Instead, the family's story of growth continued, with more land, more livestock, and more grain. Roberto's great-grandfather, Bautista, experienced further success. He passed away in 1937, leaving behind three sons—Rómulo, César (Roberto's grandfather), and Diego—and an agricultural business that carried the promise of further success. However, it was not to be for the three brothers, with one of them even going bankrupt. As the economic situation became increasingly challenging, therefore, family stories about past glories and the deeds of the early Vassolo immigrants were all but drowned out by laments regarding the privations of this new reality. How could a family that once had seemed destined for greatness now be facing such enormous adversity?

Since childhood, Roberto had heard about the business decisions made by his grandfather and his great uncles, along with their results. It would take years before he understood that their difficulties in business were strongly influenced by an environmental context that was much more challenging, in all fairness to them, than the one his great-great-grandfather had faced. His grandfather César sold products at lower, constant prices than those of the late nineteenth and early twentieth centuries. In addition to market problems, the Argentinean political authorities complicated things through their constant interventions and efforts to reallocate agricultural revenues in favor of industrial development and increasing state expenditure.

Roberto's father, who shares his first name, would observe of his visits to the farm or the local cooperative meetings: "Having debt keeps me from buying and selling when I want to, and not having that freedom is very costly in this business. I need to increase the farm's efficiency ratio, and to do that I need to increase the business's scale, but I don't have the capital to scale up. You can't do everything on your own land. It's very difficult and I don't have the capital, so I need to achieve a balance between investing in my own lands and working on leased fields."

This was when Roberto first became aware of strategic plans. Specifically, he learned from the formulation of his father's business plan in 1980, when he separated his farming operation from those of his brothers. He formally outlined and embarked on a simple strategy that combined risks with returns on investments, aimed at achieving the financial freedom to buy and sell at optimal times and operated at a scale only as large as necessary to raise his family.

For anyone who has not lived there, it might be difficult to understand the level of change and uncertainty that marked Argentina during the 1980s. From the standpoint of improving the economic lives of its citizens, it is remembered as "the lost decade." Between 1980 and 1990, per capita income remained the same. During most of the 1980s, annual inflation rates were above 100 percent, and between 1989 and 1991, there were two periods of hyperinflation.

The full realization of the original strategic plan took years. In 1995, Roberto's father informed his son that he had restored the financial health of his business. In spite of the macroeconomic turbulence of the 1980s and early 1990s, he had laid out a strategic course and established a framework for competing in the agribusiness sector and succeeding.

Was his father's strategy the reason for his success or, in such a volatile context, was luck the only explanation for the results he achieved? Was knowledge of market dynamics a factor or a differential ability to foresee or prepare for future events? Was the 1909–10 drought a random event that his ancestors were lucky to dodge but from which there is no particular lesson to be learned? Is there a fundamental rationale in natural resource industries by which organizational strategies can be outlined? How many of the bankruptcies that affected the family were the result of poor managerial decisions and how many could be attributed to external factors over which they had no influence? Working out the answers to these questions has been—and continues to be—a central feature of Roberto's research life.

SUPERCYCLES IN COMMODITY PRICES

The forces that regulate commodities pricing and production appear between the lines of this family history, with all its successes and failures. There are different types of pendular movements: annual cycles, medium-term cycles, and supercycles that last decades. Each of these cycles is brought about by a different sort of imbalance between supply and demand, and each presents distinct leadership challenges. In the following pages, we will attempt to deepen our understanding of these cycles and the imbalances that cause them in order to analyze them from the viewpoint of strategic leadership. The current section focuses on supercycles.

Supercycles are not without controversy, based as they are on statistical estimates. They attempt to predict trends in commodity prices. As econometric studies demonstrate, however, such trends are not linear but fluctuate. There is a need, therefore, to estimate both upward and downward trends. Given the intricacies and the provisional nature of the data, it is helpful to have some idea of the supercycle's estimated duration and magnitude.

Blige Erten of Northeastern University and José Antonio Ocampo of Columbia University, for example, estimated the duration of the supercycles for a wide range of commodities, identifying three great cycles. These were an upward-trending cycle that began in the second half of the nineteenth century; a downward-trending cycle that, dependent on product type, began close to the Great Depression of the 1930s; and another upward-trending cycle that began toward the end of the twentieth century and ended after the first decade of the twenty-first century, when it seems that we started another downward trend. The table offers a breakdown of these trends by commodity group.

TABLE 8.1. Duration of the supercycle in different commodity families.

Trend	Upward	Downward	Upward
Petroleum prices	1875–1925	1925–1962	1962–2010
Duration in years	50	37	48
Accumulated growth	114.2%	-32.5%	280%
Metal prices	1865–1881	1881–1974	1974–2010
Duration in years	16	93	36
Accumulated growth	1.7%	-49.2%	4.5%
Tropical agricultural commodity prices	1965–1988	1988–2002	2002–2010
Duration in years	23	114	8
Accumulated growth	16.3%	-67.2%	2.5%
Nontropical agricultural commodity prices	1889–1932	1932–1994	1994–2010
Duration in years	43	62	16
Accumulated growth	20.2%	-46.9%	6.9%

Source: Bilge Erten and José Antonio Ocampo, "Super Cycles of Commodity Prices since the Mid-Nineteenth Century," *World Development* 44 (2013): 14–30.

In a more recent study, Erten and Ocampo confirmed that global commodity prices had undergone three long-term supercycles with periodicities of thirty to forty years. They also estimate that prices are in the midst of a fourth one. They expect that the downward phase of the supercycle that started in 2014 should continue in the future, with the adverse trend being strong for oil and tropical agricultural commodities.[2]

One interesting aspect to note is the relationship between supercycles and organizational habits. For example, looking at the petroleum industry, prices have shown upward trends that continued for nearly half a century. This tendency can result in severe consequences regarding organizational habits and practices. It is the same for all of the categories. A break in these trends presents important leadership challenges when attempting to adapt the company to the new downward-trending context. Given that supercycle changes are difficult to perceive, until several years have already gone by, inevitably they pose significant strategic leadership challenges for organizational management.

We should note that some of the figures show reductions in aggregate prices. For example, nontropical agricultural prices fell 46.9 percent between 1932 and 1994. This means that, during this period, profits for any global agricultural producer would have been halved if there had been no increase in productivity. In some atypical cases, decreased prices were greatly exacerbated owing to government intervention, including the establishment of a tax on exported commodities intended to subsidize industrial development and government expenditure. To handle these situations successfully, entire organizations had to make sense of the long-term trends of commodity prices. In the case of family businesses, achieving positive economic results meant resolving ever-increasing intergenerational challenges.

Economics professor David Jacks calculated the change in prices of different commodities during certain time frames.[3] These figures supplement the work of Erten and Ocampo in the aforementioned study but involve a different estimation method. The presentation of Jacks's results is also more useful as it shows the figures reported by specific products, allowing observers to distinguish between prices of commodities in the same categories.

TABLE 8.2. Cumulative change in prices of different commodities

Commodity	1850–2011	1900–2011	1950–2011	1975–2011
Beef	155.75	96.44	214.71	-26.82
Petroleum	Not available	614.05	355.65	106.60
Corn	-39.93	-40.65	-55.90	-47.34
Wheat	-69.33	-69.93	-71.74	-59.80
Aluminum	Not available	-89.56	-42.97	-43.29
Copper	-29.51	-18.37	84.07	37.57
Potassium	Not available	-57.75	96.90	135.01
Gold	166.18	186.23	325.06	198.66
Coffee	-58.70	-46.70	-71.99	-60.51
Sugar	-86.62	-71.79	-52.57	-75.32

In addition to implicitly reflecting the cyclical nature of commodities prices, this data give a sense of the intense pressures on profit margins or the degree by which margins can increase. Long-term trends are, without a doubt, a rough measure of at least some of the strategic leadership challenges that companies will face. To fully explain these challenges, we need to examine the mechanisms behind supercycles as well as those behind the short- and medium-term changes in commodity prices. First, we will start with a long-term overview.

SUPERCYCLES AND THE DYNAMICS THAT DRIVE THEM

Commodity price cycles are driven by a dynamic created by structural factors, situational trends, and decisions made by actors from within and outside an industry. Large shifts in supply and demand influence supercycle prices. For example, the enormous growth of China since the 1980s has created so much demand in global manufacturing production that it has caused an upward trend across the natural resources sector. This is because the price of raw materials is highly correlated with the existing supply of finished products. If the production of automobiles (a finished product) increases, the demand for steel and plastic will automatically increase too. If a country has strong growth in its labor force, then, assuming there is no decrease in wages, the national demand for food will also rise.

Increased demand pushes prices up because, generally, producers cannot instantaneously increase supply. It takes time to grow crops and add to the amount of arable land available to grow them. It also takes time to discover and develop new mines and petroleum reservoirs. Even in the case of pulp and paper production, adjustments have to be made in the supply chain, and enormous capital investments have to be secured. Furthermore, lengthy feasibility studies are required, plants have to be constructed, and operational procedures need to be fine-tuned. All of this requires time.

Spikes in supply can cause supercycles. This occurs most frequently after a short period of innovation in processing technologies. The world observed an example of this in the late 1990s with the appearance of glyphosate-resistant crops along with improved direct seeding techniques that increased soy productivity. Similarly, the development of fracking technologies that facilitated the extraction of natural gas and oil reserves from sites that were thought to be exhausted increased global supplies in recent decades, while the introduction of digital controls in cellulose production boosted productivity in mills during the 1980s. We acknowledge that some of these technologies might cause severe environmental damage. The introduction of global regulations to decrease the negative impact of certain commodities and diminish global emissions from fossil energy will directly alter the supercycles.

To grasp the potential magnitude of the consequences brought about by a technological change in natural resource industries, we can consider the graph depicting the evolution of productivity in the pulp industry between 1860 and 2000.[4] The vertical axis represents productivity measured by the speed of the machines (meters per minute). We also have plotted two lines in addition to the one reflecting productivity. They estimate growth trends for periods before and after 1985. The intersection between the two lines marks the point at which there was considerable change in the productivity

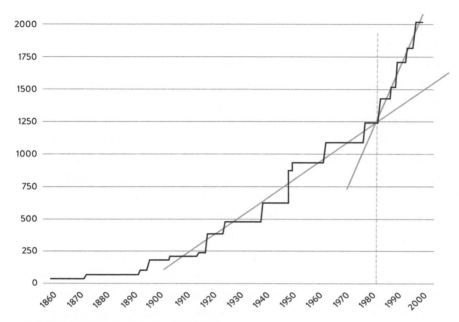

FIGURE 8.1. Productivity in the pulp industry.
Courtesy of Alfonso Cruz.

improvement rate as it began to grow along a different technological curve. This dramatic increase in the upward productivity trend is the result of the introduction of digital control.[5]

The salient question for an organization, therefore, is what do all these changes in a market or industry mean from the standpoint of competitive dynamics and strategy? When demand increases, the market's response is typically intuitive and straightforward. Once prices escalate, the number of competitors will grow, as production sites and projects that were previously considered unfeasible may eventually become attractive—with the more becoming attractive the higher that prices rise. As long as consumption rates grow faster than they did before the spike in supply, new competitors will spring up where previously there had been gaps in service. Meanwhile, those who were already in business will enjoy wider profit margins. Identifying these shifts is essential for making long-term organizational decisions and for identifying the organizational and leadership tensions to come. More of which later.

Assuming there has been no new technology that alters the dynamics, prices tend to drop when resources are dumped onto a market. Analyzing the effect of technological improvements that drive the supply is even more complicated. This is because technological improvements can simultaneously drive prices down as they increase supply and also push costs down due to the efficiency gains they generate.

After the development of fracking technology, many new competitors made their way into the petroleum industry. By contrast, innovations that resulted in higher productivity in the pulp industry spurred consolidation in the United States.[6] Determining the probable effect of downward supercycles caused by technology-driven supply spikes requires organizations to conduct in-depth sensemaking exercises.

Regulations might generate long-term movements in commodity prices. As countries shift to renewable energies and impose restrictions on fossil extraction, prices may rise. However, governmental investment in research and development in renewable energies may also prompt price reductions. The long-term price evolution is not apparent ex ante. It will depend on the combination of the global enforcement of those restrictions and the innovation investments in renewable energies.

Regardless of supercycles and their effects on organizational customs and practices, long-term price patterns involve the least volatility that these industries will experience. The strongest strategic leadership tensions will be felt more intensely during medium-term cycles and in connection with short-term volatility than at the supercycle level. In natural resource industries, price volatility emerges as the fundamental source of profit changes and, consequently, as the essential variable to incorporate in strategic thinking.

PROFIT FLUCTUATIONS

The unit price of each product sold is not the only variable that drives a company's income. Combining prices with production volumes will provide an indication of total income. But there are crucial factors that can affect this and need to be monitored. For example, what are the normal trends for the supply of raw materials? How much does demand for a given natural resource typically grow if the occasional spike is disregarded?

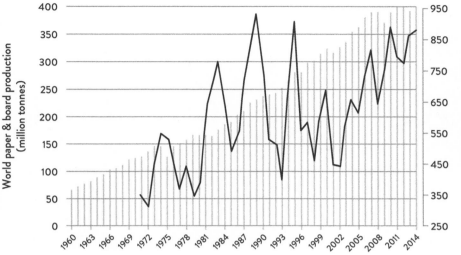

FIGURE 8.2. Evolution of pulp production and pulp prices.
Courtesy of Alfonso Cruz.

Typically, supply grows at single-digit rates, not unlike the growth rates that are seen in an industry with a differentiable product offering during its maturity. That is to say, even if prices rise and fall continuously like a roller coaster, production volumes maintain a steady course as if nothing out of the ordinary were happening.

Consider the evolution of pulp production and pulp prices as an example. Global production grew at a rate of approximately 4 percent annually between 1960 and 2014. At shorter intervals, prices rose and fell as illustrated in figure 8.2.[7]

The short-term disconnect between production volumes and market prices is striking, and alarmingly so. In most natural resource industries, increases in production and demand are relatively stable—often to the point of boredom. The exception being in cases involving severe meteorological events or war.[8] Consequently, this volatile fluctuation of prices relative to production piques the curiosity of attentive observers, especially in comparison with industries where products or services allow the existence of brand differentiation (those analyzed in the initial chapters). For example,

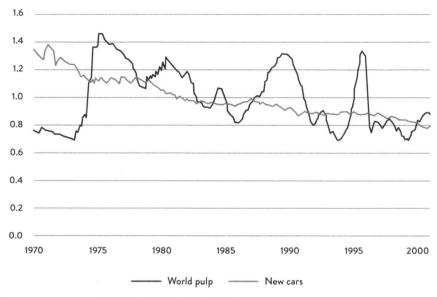

FIGURE 8.3. Evolution of wood pulp prices and car prices.
Source: Roberto S. Vassolo and Natalia Weisz.

let's examine the evolution of the pulp price with that of new cars in the United States, as plotted in figure 8.3.

What does this trend mean regarding decision-making practices for companies that compete in these industries? When production growth is stable, and price fluctuations are intense, corporate profits fluctuate drastically. Given the absence of product differentiation in commodity-based industries, a highly efficient cost structure is necessary for long-term survival. The name of the game would seem to be low costs.

A QUESTION OF COSTS IN AN INVESTMENT DECISION

The supercycle is just one of many processes that organizations competing in the natural resources sector need to master. Another is the medium-term commodity cycle. This is the consequence of simultaneous competitor investments creating price oscillations that are difficult to predict. It results in periods of excess supply for certain commodities arising from simultaneous investments in capacity, prompting drops in prices and margins. A better coordinated industry would avoid such pitfalls.

Consider the example of Arauco, one of the world-leading companies in the paper and pulp industry. In 2003, the company had to decide whether it was time to expand the operating capacity of its plant in Chile, at the cost of one billion US dollars, or to invest the same amount in the development of alternative lines of business, diversifying its interests. At the time, the price of pulp was hovering at historic lows, and most of Arauco's competitors were struggling to turn a profit.

Arauco's senior leadership team made its investment decision on the basis of a financial analysis protocol. The flow of discounted funds calculated by the pulp prices and production costs that prevailed at that time resulted in an expected value of close to zero—with every chance of that becoming a negative figure if different scenarios played out. The decision was even more challenging given that the investment of such an amount would limit the company's ability to buy new forest lands, which are essential for cellulose production. In addition to pulp, the company also had to weigh up opportunities for potential diversification investments related to wood and wood cellulose by-products.

Arauco's experience is typical of a pattern that repeats in most commodity-producing industries when product prices are low. It exemplifies how strongly the cyclical rise and fall of prices affects companies competing in commodities. If the price of wood pulp rises, the project is likely to be more profitable, but if prices drop, the project ceases to be feasible. In differentiated product industries, however, it is very likely that tight cash flow would result in immediate cancellation of investment. This especially is the case when faced with a long-term, downward trend in product prices during which costs are not expected to fall at the same rate.

A 2006 case study of Arauco,[9] published by the Harvard Business School, helps us understand how prices and projected revenues affect investment decisions. The effects are felt throughout an entire industry, shaping the competitive dynamics within it. Every player within the industry wants to know how falling prices will affect cost efficiency, their competitors, and their own comparative position. If prices drop, which companies will be worse off? Which plants are most likely to shut down? To answer these questions, Arauco needed good information on the costs of its major competitors in addition to its own.

Indisputably, in 2003, Arauco was the leader with respect to cost efficiency. The company enjoyed a substantial advantage in production costs, enabled by the tremendous growth rate of the Chilean forests and by the biological innovations the company had developed. As a result, this cost-based advantage was difficult for global competitors to imitate. Furthermore, Arauco's main competitor in Chile, CMPC, had higher general production costs owing to its own high level of diversification.

If the price of wood pulp continued to fall, other organizations in the industry would suffer losses before Arauco did. Consistent with fundamental economic theory, global production levels would decline if prices continued to drop as competitors left the market. This, in turn, would cause prices to stabilize or even rebound. The key to resolving Arauco's dilemma, therefore, was not in predicting with certainty what would happen to pulp prices. Rather, it was in anticipating the result in its competitive sphere of a worst-case price scenario in the near future. From that perspective, Arauco had a decisive advantage, substantially favoring investment in expansion of the Chilean plant's capacity.

However, in most cases, investment decisions are not so clear, and the return on such investments is dependent on other competitors' decisions that tend to be taken simultaneously. At this point, drawing up a game plan becomes exponentially more difficult. It is worth considering the contribution to game theory made by Nobel laureate John Forbes Nash to understand why this is so and to enrich our strategic thinking.

NASH'S LEGACY: GAME THEORY

Commodity cycles that oscillate for years rather than decades result from aggregate investment decisions in the industry.[10] To help managers in these industries adequately undertake investment decisions, we can draw on insights from Nash's game theory. It is worth noting, however, that Nash does not address the specific example described above. Instead, he points toward a more theoretical, potential market situation: when competitors fail to coordinate with one another, and they make simultaneous decisions, the optimum individual choice is highly likely to result in the worst collective scenario.

A typical decision for a wine producer is whether to plant grapes for red or white wine. Given that it takes a number of years for a vineyard to grow into its full production capacity, this decision is anything but trivial or insignificant. Australia, Chile, the United States, France, and Italy are all countries that have soils and natural conditions suitable for producing both red and white wine.

The proportion of lands dedicated to grapes for red or white wine changes from year to year. In the aggregate, decisions made by individuals converge and can be viewed as a single collective behavior that moves in one general direction or another. During one period, producers focus more on white wine, then on red wine, and then back to white wine again. This is another example of a pendular shift within broader natural resources fluctuations.

Consider the Australian wine industry and the percentage of total acreage dedicated to each crop, as shown in table 8.3. The back and forth displayed in the table is not the result of any supercycle, which responds to long-term structural factors. The back and forths do, however, reveal a medium-term cycle, which has a more significant connection with competitive dynamics and the coordination—or lack of it—of investment between industry participants. This appears to be what is happening with wine producers, who, in their lack of collective wisdom, continually overinvest in grape production for either red or white wine. Eventually, this causes a drop in the price of the overproduced type and an increase in the price of the underproduced type.

To sketch this out in another industrial setting, when a company like Arauco decides to expand its plant, the effect is twofold: it adds production capacity to a business where competition is governed by costs, and also may push prices further down due to a potential oversupply of wood pulp. The reaction of a competitor can further accelerate the downturn or can alleviate it, depending on whether the competitor decides to also invest or to postpone investments. The industrial cycle, therefore, will be partially determined by these decisions.

TABLE 8.3. Evolution of red and white wine grapes—percentage of total acreage dedicated to each crop in Australia.

Period	1955–1956	1965–1966	1974–1977	1984–1987	1994–1997	1999–2000
Red	32.6	26.9	39.7	27.0	33.4	44.0
White	67.4	73.1	60.3	73.0	66.6	56.0

Source: Authors' own preparation with information gathered from the Australian Wine and Brandy Association.

Because investments in natural resources take years to come to fruition, and because the product is homogeneous, information about current prices can actually interfere with making decisions about the future. If prices are rising, many competitors are likely to expedite approval of projects such as replacing old plants in orchards or vineyards with new ones. It is very possible that several competitors will make separate investment decisions concurrently. Again, high prices draw new players into a given market. However, getting started with a new product in the natural resources sector generally means eliminating one crop, replacing it with another, and then waiting a few years. Because higher prices typically trigger investment decisions and often occur simultaneously, investments by diverse producers also typically begin to yield returns during similar time frames. This produces a surplus of raw materials that hastens a decline in prices and may force plants or companies out of the market—again, more or less, at the same time.

Owing to a fall in crude oil prices during 2015 and 2016, many shale oil and shale gas companies in the United States either went into liquidation or sought court protection while they attempted to mount a recovery. Most of these companies had come into the market only a few years earlier when crude prices were booming. Their collective mistake was to base investment decisions on prices that prevailed at the moment of investment without considering the actions of other competitors.

When facing such decisions, the challenge is to anticipate the movements of the rest of the industry and, often, to temporarily pursue a countercyclical strategy, separating oneself from the herd's behavior. Such countercyclical strategies often require making investments during periods of low rather than high prices. When managers observe a high level of industry investment and high commodity prices, it is worth revisiting investment decisions. For instance, if the primary decision assessment uses net present value (or similar valuation tools), we recommend sensitizing future cash flows by commanding low price scenarios. This is easy to implement but is very difficult to sustain, especially when human pressures demand short-term results on top of the already difficult task of making predictions and evaluating when to sell a product.

IN THE SHADOW OF SPECULATION

In natural resource industries, episodes of market disequilibrium are influenced by the buzz of short-term speculation in raw materials. In addition to being goods that can be marketed in response to various needs, commodities can function as stores of value. To varying degrees, their properties are similar to those of money in that they serve as units of measure, units of exchange, and as strategic reserves. These have allowed for the creation of countless derivative financial investment instruments backed by commodities. To give an idea of the prevalence of commodities-based financial transactions, a unit of the commodity is often bought and sold more than ten times before reaching the consumer. Given how common these financial exchanges are, raw materials prices are subject to dynamics that are often unrelated to the supply-side and demand-side factors that directly affect the price of the underlying commodity—in both the short and long term. Price expectations and arbitrage opportunities introduce other external factors that influence commodity prices.

Natural resource industries also can be politically sensitive. For example, the United States regulates the domestic oil market for reasons of national security. This artificially affects prices. Elsewhere, the Argentinean government more than once has introduced controls on the supply of grains and meat, playing politics with and generating taxes from the food industry, while the Canadian government established the Canadian Wheat Board as the only legal purchaser of wheat and barley in most of western Canada as a means of counteracting trading oligopolies.

Amid all these factors potentially affecting prices, the predominance of cycles driven by market forces remains the rule. Moreover, while academics can study long-lasting supercycles by use of approximations and draw conclusions that are useful from practical and strategic perspectives, in everyday terms, competing in natural resource industries means being bound to constant price fluctuations. This creates significant leadership tension, as many essential business decisions cannot be framed in terms of quarters and years, but in multiyear periods of price uncertainty. We must not forget that this occurs in the context of industries with millennia-long histories, which can give the false impression that competing in these industries is straightforward.

BETWEEN SMALL STEPS AND GIANT LEAPS

In December 2014, North Farming, a family business that held several thousand hectares of land in northern Argentina, started to develop a new strategy. The family was growing. This made it necessary to generate new business interests, to reorganize the already-complex company, and to determine the factors that would drive growth. Over the preceding years, the company had experienced many challenges in connection with its production of crops and livestock. As a result, the company had started to diversify, aggressively pursuing vertical integration. It had set up new business lines such as food product storage, shipping, feed-milling, and more.

In a directors' meeting held that December, Norberto Quiroga, the family patriarch and founder of the business, addressed a group of sixteen people, including family and nonfamily members with managerial positions. He projected the company's asset development history on screen. It showed positive leaps in most years. His speech had a single objective: to point out that there were two particular years that accounted for most of the company's growth: one was the year when a revaluation of their lands in the Salta province took place, and the other was the year their livestock was revalued.

This produced a feeling of ambivalence among the attendees. A significant proportion of the company's asset growth could not be attributed to sound management or performance but to two incidents that, while not totally unforeseen, were almost uncontrollable in terms of businesses development. Just as was the case with the Vassolo family during the great drought of 1909–10, there was a realization that, after decades of hard work and struggle, the company's gain and loss of wealth depended much more on limited, time-bound events rather than on the aggregate of their year-to-year activities.

In 1908, the Vassolo family's problem was fundamentally one that required an intertemporal solution—one in which an actor's present-day decisions affect the future options available. There was no way the family could have known of the approaching drought, but they did understand business cycles and the opportunity to transform one type of asset into another, even if doing so meant increased financial stress in the short term. They understood that selling livestock was essentially cutting off an income-generating mechanism in exchange for a promise that the land itself would return the investment and yield additional income at some indeterminate time in the future.

In 2014, Quiroga's family faced a similar situation. It was, perhaps, somewhat more predictable in the sense that the family could study the evolution of the livestock cycle and, to some degree, anticipate when prices would increase. Nonetheless, both stories illustrate a fundamental fact of business dependent on natural resources: a large part of the game consists of sustaining the company until particularly large leaps in the value of assets occur so that the company can monetize their value after years of patiently waiting.

THE KEYS TO SUCCESS IN NATURAL RESOURCES

There are three elements that determine the success or failure of a company's strategic plan when competing in natural resources: its cost structure, arbitrage, and financial flexibility.[11] More importantly, these three elements are interrelated.

As the first key to success, *low costs* are synonymous with success in natural resource businesses. Achievement of low costs is the result of operational efficiency and careful attention to management and productive structures. One can scarcely conceive of successfully competing in natural resource industries without making a mantra out of operational efficiency. There are various means for achieving it. For instance, sometimes it stems from a management-level focus on production processes, at others from effectively handling the outsourcing of noncore activities.

Cost efficiencies play a huge role in determining the earnings of a natural resources company. The other factor that determines profits is the maximization of sales prices combined with the minimization of purchasing prices. Because these prices fluctuate within a given fiscal year, maximizing the buy-sell spread—or arbitrage—managing when to purchase and when to sell, will lead to better outcomes on financial statements at the year's end.

Arbitrage is a concept with which managers are familiar. Why, therefore, does it often prove so difficult a process for companies to manage? The first reason is the degree of uncertainty involved. Even though it is possible to anticipate the cyclical fluctuations, it is impossible to know definitively whether an upward or downward price trend will continue. However, the main difficulty is, generally, the cost of arbitrage. In order to wait for the optimal time, a company must have a strong financial backbone and a degree of financial flexibility, as it seeks out better relative prices.

At its core, managing arbitrage is an adaptive challenge. Immobilizing capital for flexibility competes with shareholders' interest in receiving dividends and with employees' interest in higher salaries and bonuses. Arbitrage occurs outside of annual cycles. It can manifest itself in the commodities business in simple forms, such as holding a product for a few months until the optimal season for sales. But arbitrage can also occur inter-annually, necessitating a wait for the best time to invest in a mine, to acquire a vineyard, or to purchase more livestock. For some commodities, the wait for the right price dynamics can take decades and, therefore, requires major decisions regarding business viability and longevity.

Consequently, while the different types of cycles obey regular patterns, adjusting the capabilities of companies to take advantage of these evolutionary trends does introduce substantial adaptive leadership challenges. This is particularly the case when the different cycles shift trends in an unsynchronized manner. This is the subject of the next chapter.

CHAPTER 9

NAVIGATING THE STRUCTURAL CHALLENGE

The exercise of leadership when commodity prices decrease is uniquely complex owing to the competing mechanisms that guide the evolution of prices. Estimating the long-term price trends is much more difficult than during the developmental challenge, which brings with it its own challenges and affects sensemaking capabilities. The existence of simultaneous underlying commodity cycles makes it particularly difficult to diagnose the structural challenge. In this chapter, we dig into the difficulties of navigating this challenge.

EXERCISING LEADERSHIP IN LIGHT OF INTERTEMPORAL TENSIONS

The first step toward exercising strategic leadership in such situations is to conduct *systemic observation* through a unique set of lenses adjusted to the dynamics of businesses based on natural resources. In general, expenditure and costs shoot up during periods of high prices, and dreams are snuffed out in periods of low prices. This occurs across entire organizations.

Strategic leadership requires having to constantly maneuver within these intertemporal tensions in order to improve systemic diagnoses, conflictual interpretations, and adaptive interventions.

As a good illustration of leadership tensions that apply specifically to natural resource companies, we can look at the challenges faced by Codelco, Chile's largest copper mining company, in connection with the fluctuations of its production costs. As copper had a relatively high value during the first decade of this century, there had been less emphasis on cost efficiency. As a result, production costs in some Codelco divisions had risen to over US $3 per pound. However, by the end of 2015, global copper prices had declined to $2.13 per pound. This left several divisions operating at a loss. Many of these units had low productivity, which was a structural problem for Codelco. However, problems like these can sometimes cloud an assessment. Wage hikes primarily caused the spike in costs as wages rose in tandem with copper prices, ultimately surpassing them.

As copper prices began to fall, this became an explosive topic at the meetings of Codelco's senior management team. Timely systemic observation would likely have eased the effects of the later debate, identifying the existence of the problem while copper prices were still high. Postponing discussions of this type until prices had begun to drop only made managing the situation more difficult. Decisions that increased costs had already been made, and it was much harder to scale them back than it was to approve them. To deal with these tensions proactively, leadership had to understand that they were generated by adaptive challenges and had a substantial incubation period long before they surfaced.

The next step in the adaptation-oriented strategic leadership process is *conflictual interpretation*. Again, the most advisable approach here is to focus on organizational pain caused by losses. In contrast to industries with differentiable products, essential organizational capacities in natural resource industries do not differ dramatically from one stage of its cycle to another. Therefore, in general, distress caused by direct losses predominates over the pain caused by losses of competencies in natural resource businesses. Capacity losses are far less significant for the cyclical challenges faced by natural resource companies than for those that face transformative or creative challenges. This is not to say that capacity losses will never occur. Indeed, they might, especially after several years of financial security. However, the nature of the work does not change significantly enough between stages of a cycle to make this dimension as necessary in this industry as it can be in others.

Expansive cycles often result in permanent increases in the personal spending levels of all types of organizational expenditures among the various stakeholders. When margins begin to shrink, this is frequently the cause of a great deal of tension, as management attempts to adjust salary levels downward. Further, much of the resistance the organization will experience comes from factions that are outside the organization. Tackling this problem involves managing direct losses in many other organizations that do business with the company. It will be hardest for those who have more significant economic needs and, usually, less negotiating power.

Adaptive intervention should not be undertaken with a uniform approach. It must be managed differently depending on the cycle and, very importantly, during any periods indicating shifts in a cyclical trend. During periods of escalating prices, all stakeholders will demand a greater share of the differential revenue. During peaks, the natural tendency will be to acquiesce to these demands, instead of confronting them. The system can do so in the short term without frustrating any of the factions. However, the extent to which a company gives in to these demands will inevitably determine the extent of its suffering as the cycle's trend reverses.

Mobilizing the organization from a position of authority involves pushing it to recognize and acknowledge the system's intertemporal challenges and to deal with them reasonably. However, organizational systems will not react unless tension levels are elevated. The fundamental question to pose to the system during periods of high prices will center on the organization's sustainability during periods of low prices. Necessarily, leadership should ask organizational factions to evaluate scenarios focused on such questions as: "What would it mean for our organization to have prices revert to the historical average?"

Even in good times, the whole organization should understand that the company's financial situation is entirely different when the price cycle reverses and enters a period shaped by low commodity prices. Making mistakes while implementing solutions, or avoiding the issues altogether, can be fatal for the aspirations of many stakeholders.

Times of low prices must be managed carefully with regard to the organization's identity and purpose. For what reasons are we asking the organization to diligently and continually transform its routines to achieve greater efficiency over time? How do we inspire all personnel to share in this vision? The organization, inclusive of leadership and lower-level personnel, will have to address and uncover this together. Failure to generate greater efficiency will result in the company losing talent and, with it, organizational competencies. It will be, as a consequence, in a weaker competitive position by the time prices do bounce back.

THE TRAP OF FALSE SIMPLICITY

If you are not competing in a natural resource industry and you are thinking of investing in one, it is worth considering that the "simplicity" of the key success factors does not itself mean that doing business in these industries is "simple." In fact, to make such an assumption could be a lethal trap. We faced this trap even with very successful managers of other types of industries. We particularly remember one of our clients, Florencia Vazquez.

Florencia was the president of Cap Legal Services and had invested much of her primary business's profits in developing a model agricultural project. She was particularly sensitive to employee needs and to environmental concerns. The company paid its personnel very well in the different business units, even above the standard of the legal services industry, and much above the agricultural levels. In light of environmental concerns, Florencia pushed managers from the agriculture business unit to give special consideration to the sustainable development of the land, with an emphasis on longer crop rotation and soil resting periods. However, after years of significant investments, the company was still a long way off achieving its goal. The drop in agricultural commodity prices in 2014 and 2015 made those years particularly complicated and had greatly diminished the company's earnings.

Florencia was the eldest sister and the president of her family's successful legal service sector business. She had great entrepreneurial ability and extensive experience of legal service industries, yet it was nearly impossible for her to maintain a dialogue about improving profitability with her agricultural manager. He responded to every proposal with some reference to the external context, such as falling commodities prices, drought, heavy rains, or the lack of financial freedom. He would recite an endless list of causes unrelated to the business that allegedly explained the poor results. Florencia found this baffling.

The failure of the agricultural operations to produce profits, however, was rooted in salary levels and decisions regarding vertical integration that made the business unsustainable during periods of low prices. While reorganizing in order to decrease the total burden of salaries and capital expenditure, the outsourcing of some of the value chain activities was particularly challenging in light of the success in the other business units. Florencia felt that applying a different rationale to commodities than to other business units was a sign of disloyalty to the rest of the organization and its culture.

We met Florencia after being consulted about strategic planning for the legal business unit. When the topic of the agricultural operations came up, we decided to put it off for another time. Florencia's face belied the intense bitterness and frustration she felt, practically to the point that it began to affect her self-esteem.

Over the years, we have encountered many cases like this. The allure of agribusiness is irresistible for many Latin American businesspeople, perhaps due to a regional attachment to the land, or perhaps because agribusiness appears simple at a superficial level, like something that can be managed in one's spare time or on weekends. We call this misconception *the trap of false simplicity*.

This trap arises from an objective reality: viewed from the outside, the managerial tasks relating to natural resources are relatively straightforward and repetitive. However, as we have discussed, the logic of a successful business model in these industries differs significantly from those whose main product allows for brand differentiation. When diversifying in these industries, it is fundamental to keep in mind these differences, otherwise the risk of failure increases substantially.

VERTICAL INTEGRATION AS WORK AVOIDANCE

Several successful managers competing in natural resource industries tend to underscore the challenge of diversifying in other sectors. The impulse to grow is part of the DNA of many businesses, making it difficult to set aside the belief that, each year, the organization needs to be bigger than the previous one. There are, in fact, many ways to grow in a company based on natural resources. It is possible to break through the commodities price ceiling by producing and marketing services or products with particular characteristics. For example, high-protein soybeans bring an increased price, just as does low-sulfur oil.

At times, the way to break free from the restrictions that commodity production can impose is by extending the reach of the organization's ownership into the value chain, pursuing vertical integration, just as Cap Legal Services did in the agriculture business unit. Determining to what extent an organization should integrate vertically is a challenge involving both technical and adaptive aspects. For these reasons, it is common to find extremely diverse levels of vertical integration within a single sector.

For example, during the era of classical Hollywood cinema in the 1930s and early 1940s, studios had writers, directors, cinematographers, editors, and actors on contract; they owned the lots on which the films were written, shot, and edited; they owned the theaters in which the films were shown. In effect, they had a monopoly on the means of production, distribution, and exhibition. They were vertically integrated—a situation that changed dramatically in the postwar period with the landmark 1948 US Supreme Court decision on an antitrust case against the major studios.

Oil companies are another example of how organizations in one industry often choose to integrate to varying degrees. The different stages of the oil and gas value chain are exploration, production, storage and shipping, refining, and marketing. The terms upstream, midstream, and downstream are often used to refer to the major sectors or operational components of the petroleum industry.

The upstream operational components, also known as exploration and production (E&P), involve the exploration for and extraction of crude oil and natural gas. It includes the search for potential underground or underwater oil and gas fields, the drilling of exploratory wells, and the operation of wells that bring crude oil and natural gas to the surface. The midstream operational components involve storing, marketing, and transporting crude oil, natural gas, by-product sulfur, and natural gas liquids such as ethane, propane, and butane. The downstream involves the refining of crude oil and the processing of natural gas. It includes the selling and distribution of processed natural gas and the products derived from crude oil such as liquified petroleum gas (LPG), gasoline (or petrol), jet fuel, diesel oil, other fuel oils, petroleum asphalt, and petroleum coke. Overall, it includes petroleum refineries, petroleum product distribution, retail outlets, and natural gas distribution companies.

While some concentrate exclusively on exploration and production, there are others that reach far into downstream activities like operating their own service stations. For example, the Argentinean oil company Pluspetrol has a primary focus on exploration, whereas Petrobras, a Brazilian firm, has an extremely high level of vertical integration and undertakes many different activities up and down the value chain, from exploration to managing retail service stations.

Few pulp companies could rival Arauco in the year 2003. Most were extensively diversified, with many producing consumer goods made from pulp, such as certain types of furniture. Even its main competitor in Chile, CMPC, was significantly more vertically integrated than Arauco or its largest worldwide competitors like the Finnish Stora Enso or the American International Paper.

Any vertical integration strategy is potentially valid. However, each must be evaluated with great care. When a natural resource company feels pressure to engage in vertical integration, it should first undertake a systemic assessment of the organization using the adaptive leadership framework. De-commoditizing a business involves reaching into industries where competition is dominated by the logic of product differentiation (as explained in relation to the developmental challenge and the creative challenge). The competitive dynamics in natural resource industries are so distinct from those of differentiated products that one could say that these firms have a distinct DNA. Often, the degree to which a different mindset is required is seldom anticipated.

What Heifetz and Linsky termed *work avoidance* is evident in organizations with lackluster results. Instead of seeking to achieving excellence in core operations, bolstering existing business, companies have a tendency to embark on unfamiliar paths. This shift in focus either conceals or ignores any number of core operational failures. In other words, the failure to overcome the structural challenge is the result of avoiding the distress provoked by the problem and the changes it demands. Holding on to past assumptions, externalizing the problem, denying it, or bypassing it with a distracting (but ultimately ineffective) solution may temporarily restore stability. This is less stressful than facing up to and taking responsibility for the demands of the structural challenge. In many cases, diversification through vertical integration serves as a distracting solution. The system maintains itself by avoiding the necessary adaptive work. This might result in two unintended consequences: neither the core business nor the new business delivers the expected results.

It is essential, therefore, that during an adaptive intervention designed to assess the desirability of vertical integration, management deliberations must focus on the central themes as reiteratively as necessary, putting front and center of the discussion the real motives behind the decision. For what reasons are we seeking to expand our activities along the value chain? Are we seeking to enhance capacities or just running away from our incompetence in the core business? This last question is particularly tricky as it requires that people recognize their deficiencies and commit to their resolution. One of the most important questions to consider, even though it seems to run counter to the financial investment logic that currently dominates in the business world, is whether it is, in fact, essential to grow at a certain annual rate. Indeed, it is the unthinking acceptance of this logic that often compels organizations to seek horizontal or vertical integration whenever commodities prices fall and growth rates decline.

A SPECIFIC DNA

The intrinsic difference between the strategic leadership challenges, discussed in the previous chapters of this book, and structural challenges, such as those facing natural resources companies, is that, generally, the other changes can be managed as they occur. For companies in industries with product differentiation, strategic leadership challenges are one-time events for a particular business unit, although organizations may experience more than one in their lifetime—which becomes more likely the more as a company's level of diversification increases.

Life is different for natural resources organizations that must deal with structural challenges. The recurrence of low-price, high-pressure periods demands constant questioning regarding what is the most sustainable level of expenditure. By this point, the reader may have observed our conviction that confronting structural challenges, essentially, means cultivating an organization with a DNA designed to engage in continuous intertemporal questioning concerning the organization's structural decisions.

This should not be confused with what Heifetz and Linsky call *adaptive DNA organizations*, a term they use to describe organizations with an active practice of resolving their challenges adaptively, which is something that all organizations, ideally, can develop. While these concepts are not in conflict, we refer here to a specific character trait that should be ingrained within the culture of companies facing structural challenges: the ability to focus the organizational discussion on the fact that business will always be subject to a contextual framework of product price cycles.

A company's entrance into a period of increasing prices should not destroy an organization's practice of intertemporal questioning but instead should strengthen it. Thinking about long-term cost structures is less of a strain during the good times. In this sort of internal environment, all cyclical changes in prices will be pointed reminders of what the important tasks are in these types of organization, but this is especially so with downward price trends.

When senior management has developed a DNA for intertemporal questioning, organizational development becomes a much more positive and attractive task, even during times of increased pressure on profit margins. The degree to which this practice has been institutionalized will be reflected by periodic organizational meetings and, more broadly, in the structuring of the organization's business model. It materializes in the firm's culture and values. The DNA helps to maintain a strategic position that is ever mindful of how recurring price cycles pressure the development of the organization and its personnel. Whenever this DNA is at risk of being compromised, those in authority must urgently design adaptive interventions to restore it.

BRIEF GUIDE
to Spotting and Responding
to Structural Challenge

SCAN THE EXTERNAL ENVIRONMENT
Anticipate Price Declines

When operating in a natural resource industry, the first thing to scan is the trend in your product prices. For this, you need to differentiate short-term from middle-term and long-term cycles. Within the year, you will observe price fluctuations, but these are not the ones that matter most in terms of organizational structure. Monitor the level of investments in your industry. If you observe simultaneous investments in your industry, you can anticipate the Nash coordination problem. There is likely to be excess supply over the coming years and a price decline as these investments result in full production.

You need to anticipate the evolution of supercycles by analyzing long-term consumer demand, supply chains, the emergence of new producers, and technological innovation. Indicators that prices will drop in the mid- to long term require progression to the next step.

Conjecture on the Optimal Organization Size and Cost Structures under the New Conditions

When prices begin to decline, the name of the game is to ensure cost efficiency relative to your competitors. As such, you need to answer two essential questions. First, what cost structure will be necessary to survive under the new conditions? Second, what is the optimal size for the business to attain the required cost structure? Continuous benchmarking of the cost structure is fundamental to answer these questions. Besides, you need to assess: Do assets require reconfiguration? Is there a need to adopt new technology or change production skills? Is it necessary to reduce head count?

SCAN THE INTERNAL ENVIRONMENT— MAKE INTERPRETATIONS—MOBILIZE

Observe the Inner Tensions and Reactions among Different Functional Groups

You are trying to detect if your organization mimics the changes in the external environment, indicating that you face a structural challenge. Remember that the strategic imperative is cost efficiency. As you proceed, you are likely to encounter work avoidance mechanisms when analyzing cost structures or organizational efficiency. Unions usually react against salary adjustments that are linked to new prices. Different organizational factions complain about both authority figures and external factors. Management teams often start searching for diversification alternatives that do not solve organizational cost and efficiency problems.

Analyze and Question the Rationale behind New Business Opportunities

Your company will have multiple growth opportunities. However, a typical task-evasion behavior is to rush into vertical integration or unrelated diversification in order to delay cost reduction decisions. The senior management team should ensure that the current business is sustainable in the long term while also exploring growth opportunities.

Address Direct Losses

In the context of structural changes, direct losses have higher importance, relatively speaking, than in other challenges. The structural challenge means facing resource scarcity in the long run, and this necessarily implies direct losses. The senior management team needs to create holding environments in which to discuss the scope of the adjustment. The annual strategic planning meeting is a useful opportunity to address these losses and their contextualization in relation to future objectives and aspirations.

Engage the Different Departments in Looking Forward
The structural challenge has different implications for different departments. To ease the effect of the structural challenge on the direct losses for different groups, senior management teams need to foster the creation of holding environments where departments can dream in the future. Engage in group studies of different cyclical scenarios and pose "what if?" questions. Create situations for analyzing future events and develop a DNA for intertemporal questioning. Query whether the real motivation behind internal pressures toward vertical integration lies in sound strategic thinking or work avoidance.

CHAPTER 10

LEADING THROUGH CONCURRENT CHALLENGES

What could be worse than facing one strategic challenge? Facing two challenges simultaneously. So, what could be worse than that? Facing three challenges at the same time. This is not a hypothetical situation that we are talking about, but something real that has a dramatic effect given the combinatory impact of the different challenges. In fact, one of the salient characteristics of the strategic leadership challenges is that they often arrive simultaneously. A fundamental skill for members of a senior management team, therefore, is the ability to detect the convergence of these challenges and put in place a strategy to tackle them.

NOT EVERYTHING IS TRIGGERED BY THE ENVIRONMENT

This book is about helping you to detect, sort, order, articulate, and put into effect a strategy to address business realities. By this stage, you should be prepared to rapidly diagnose and respond to different situations, often triggered by environmental change. There remains, however, one final situation for us to consider, as exemplified by Gerardo's story.

Gerardo Cech acted as the head of Pampa Construction Inc., a family business that provides different construction services for midsized projects in Argentina. When he first came to see us, Gerardo was worried about the company's profitability and its managers' unwillingness to assume full accountability for their own work. Each service category manager appeared to have created their own comfortable kingdom within the functional area for which they were responsible and demonstrated a lack of concern for the company's falling profit margins. Gerardo felt he had clearly communicated the importance of accountability, having emphasized the importance of taking into consideration the entire stakeholder community in all decision-making. Given his emphasis on this issue, the managers' lackluster reaction left him disconcerted.

As a result of our knowledge of the market, we knew the construction sector in the country was going through a difficult time. Our first assumption was that the circumstances might indicate that companies in the industry could be going through a developmental challenge. However, this particular challenge was notably different from those we have described in the previous chapters.

A few pieces of the puzzle were distinct from the situation we normally observe in developmental challenges. We were mostly surprised by the lack of concern displayed by managers for some of the company's fundamental values. The main issue did not appear to be resistance to the shift from a focus on sales to a focus on margins (typical of the developmental challenge, as we discussed in chapter 2). Which is not to say, however, that such resistance was not in evidence. Rather, the principal concern involved the discomfort of preserving operational autonomy within a framework of greater coordination.

As we continued our conversation, additional dynamics began to appear. Gerardo, who headed the organization and presided over the board, summarized the most important events of the last few years for us. His father had taken action to ensure he was fully trained in and comprehended the business. Indeed, in one form or another, he had participated in the family business since adolescence and had gone on to study for a master's degree in business administration at a prestigious university.

Gerardo understood the company's clients very well and was clear about its key success factors.

As the business grew, the family faced a complex decision. Gerardo could not closely supervise all the business units. This had prompted him, five years before our consultation, to withdraw from operations and focus on directing the board and supervising the leaders of the distinct business units. Gerardo saw this as a necessary step to professionalize the business, with managers taking on responsibility for day-to-day decision-making, while family board members addressed high-level, strategic matters and broad oversight of the business.

As a result of our discussion, we saw that Gerardo had gone too far with his decision to protect a core organizational value, encouraging managerial autonomy. The distinct business units had become isolated from one another, lacking sufficient coordination and interoperability. We began to see that the adverse events that were affecting the entire industry were not the main source of organizational tensions. That is, the origin of the problem did not lie in the developmental challenge the company was facing. Instead, environmental changes reinforced the existence of an inadequate organizational design that would have resulted in severe problems even in the absence of any environmental changes.

ORGANIZATIONAL DEVELOPMENT AND DEVELOPMENT OF THE MARKET

Up to this point, our book has depended on outside-in analysis. This is the reason we speak of *strategic* leadership challenges. The adjective *strategic* signals that the origin of a particular challenge arises from phenomena enveloping the entire sector in which the company competes, not from within the company itself. The outside-in analysis helps the senior management team to both realize the type of strategic priority the company will need to establish and the type of organizational losses these priorities will entail. However, the reality is that all organizations simultaneously have to address external (outside-in) and internal (inside-out) factors, which affect business dynamics and organizational development. It is important to recognize the genesis of these distinct processes in order to put in proper perspective the specifics of the strategic leadership challenge.

Strategic change specialist Larry Greiner has identified the existence of internal processes in organizations that occur over long periods of time.[1] Both the passage of time and the growth in the size of a business inevitably result in the emergence of new challenges that organizations have to confront. These challenges force companies to find new ways of organizing. In the case of Gerardo's company, the family's management was successful while the family directly supervised core operations. As the business grew, however, it required a new management system, involving different styles and processes. The industry to which it belonged may not have been going through any significant changes, but the company's greater size meant that the organizational design that had brought success in the first instance was no longer adequate.

For Greiner, organizations must design custom-made solutions to meet many of their needs. However, the same organizational practices cannot endure indefinitely. They need to be updated in light of changes in organizational size and age. Management problems and principles, in fact, are rooted in time. The concept of decentralization, for example, can describe corporate practices at one period but can lose its descriptive power at another. The passage of time is a factor, therefore, in understanding company size.

In the same vein, a company's organizational design for dealing with problems and stating solutions tends to change markedly as the number of its employees and its sales volume increase. The reason is that the difficulties of coordination and communication are magnified in proportion to organization scale. Inevitably, as a company grows, new functions emerge, levels in the management hierarchy multiply, and different jobs become more interrelated.

Companies that do not grow can retain many of the same management practices over long periods. Companies that do grow, however, need to constantly review and adapt their practices.

The appropriate organizational solution in any given case will be driven by the organization's most dominant needs. Consider the example of formal organizational structure. When a company grows and its business units assume importance in and of themselves, the formal structure begins to strain under the pressure. In general, it is necessary in such a situation to change from a functional organizational model to a divisional model. Similarly, when a company has grown across several countries, formal structures organized by geography tend to become insufficient. Matrix-based structures are often necessary to unify an organization's separate business units and activities across locations.

Organizations tend to experience high levels of stress when they transition to new structural models. While things are going well, there are periods of evolution during which there are incremental adjustments to the formal structure. But as time passes and the company size increases, the organizational structure soon becomes obsolete. The company will then have to undergo a period of revolution. It is forced to find a new design, modifying everything: its formal structure, its managerial and evaluative systems, and its central processes and management style. The entire organization experiences doubt and uncertainty. While this is an adaptive leadership challenge, it does not constitute a strategic leadership challenge in the way we have defined that term in this book.

Change processes happen simultaneously in different parts of organizations and obey their own internal logic. However, they cannot be divorced entirely from events taking place in the external business context. The interplay between the two generates an additional challenge when it comes to assessing the source of organizational problems. Moreover, the lack of coherence between the size of an organization and its structural design becomes more evident and acute when it is forced to confront complex industry-wide problems at the same time as undergoing internal change. In the case of the Pampa Construction Inc., Gerardo changed its structure to enable delegation and autonomous decision-making. Nonetheless, this was not the right solution for the company at that time. Although the problems dated back to the company's modification of its organizational structure, they came fully to a head during a period of financial crisis.

THE PERFECT STORM

In October 1991, Hurricane Grace appeared to be running out of steam near Sable Island, having cut a trajectory through the Caribbean and northward toward Atlantic Canada. However, its collision with both a low-pressure system and a cold front reinvigorated the dying hurricane, generating what became known as the "Perfect Storm." There are frequent parallels in the world of business. During a company's lifespan, the intersection of numerous issues and challenges can render an industrial "perfect storm" a real possibility.

A typical example of such a scenario occurs when a national recession coincides with an industry's transition from the developmental stage to maturity. This is exactly what happened to the global cellular communications industry during 2008 and 2009. In chapter 1 and chapter 2, we saw that the challenge faced by Laura García and Bestclearing Inc. was very much focused on the successful navigation of a perfect storm. As her industry's growth slowed dramatically, the entire Latin American region began to enter a recession. To make matters worse, there was an ongoing debate within her company regarding the viability of the organizational structure it had adopted during the previous decade in response to the region's economic growth.

It is the senior management team's task to navigate a company through the white noise of a perfect storm, during which everything can appear to be an urgent problem that has to be addressed now. In order to prioritize what should be addressed and in what sequence, it is necessary to identify the changes, organizational processes, and external context that together affect the company in a perfect storm. Fundamentally, the senior management team must be on the lookout for signs and objective data indicating that evolutionary forces are at work in the surrounding environmental context.

In the case of Bestclearing Inc., the firm was involved in both a developmental challenge and an emergency challenge. What is more, it appeared to be undergoing the type of long-term structural change Greiner described. In these circumstances, senior management should have started to generate hypotheses and to evaluate them collaboratively with their teams while maintaining control of the overall process. The sooner the effects of the recession could be understood separately from the effects caused by maturation of the industry, the sooner the company could determine how much stress was the result of organizational design change and how much arose from outside-in factors. It was essential that both the developmental and the emergency challenges were taken into consideration.

This type of problem becomes even more complex if an internal organizational development issue emerges during a transition but is actually caused by unresolved organizational design problems, especially when the problem has been covered up by excess cash and profits earned during periods of expansion. When this third type of problem is present, the risk of failure in connection with managing the leadership challenges takes on even greater significance. It becomes all the more necessary that senior management teams develop an awareness of the severity of the coming storm. But it is also important to know how to take full advantage of the calmer times, preparing for the future and the unexpected.

THE ART OF CAPITALIZING ON ECONOMIC BOOMS

At the time of writing, it is over twenty-eight years, dating back to 1991, since Australia experienced a technical recession; that is, two consecutive quarters of negative growth.[2] This has been the largest period of expansion in the country's history, with Australia surpassing the Netherlands in holding the global record for consecutive years of growth. For such countries, familiarity with ongoing, long-term growth can make it seem like a permanent fixture. This is far from the truth. While these can appear to be wonderful times, they are also extremely dangerous.

Periods of organizational expansion have a seductive force and generally are aspired to by senior management teams. During boom times, they can satisfy the urge to grow, "change the world," and be paid well in the process. Sales increase, the bottom line is healthy, and every day the organization takes on more and better talent to take charge of different organizational processes. If the economy of its home country is also growing and developing, then it is likely that people from all over the world will choose that country as a place to make a life for themselves, further adding to the potential pool of talent.

In chapter 3, we considered a boom phenomenon in terms of the development of an industry centered on differentiated products. We described this as a linear process that ends with businesses in a given industry facing a developmental challenge. There are, however, other types of booms. For instance, those that correspond to businesses dominated by cyclical changes, such as those seen in natural resource industries or in macroeconomics.

All booms are similar in that organizations experience the same temptation to overfocus on the short term. When a boom begins to wane and short and recurrent contractions are observed, organizations will face a plethora of distinct strategic leadership dilemmas. Consequently, their management teams will also need to draw on an array of mobilizing interventions.

PREDICTING RECESSIONS

The occurrence of recessions is a sure thing. Sooner or later economic growth stops. Even in the Australian case, some scholars argue that the absence of recessions is more a problem of definition than a reflection of fact. The conventional definition of a recession is two or more consecutive quarters of falling real GDP. Since the population has grown rapidly in Australia, this has sustained the GDP growth. However, if we measure the recession in terms of per-capita contraction (two or more quarters), Australia was in recession in the September and December quarters of 2000, the March and June quarters of 2006, and the September and December quarters of 2018.

We also know that recessions will differ in their magnitude and duration. Which raises the question: is it possible to predict future occurrences without being an economic expert? Economists sometimes joke, "I have successfully predicted 10 of the last 5 recessions." In that light, and given that experts cannot agree on the probability of any future recession, what can we do as businesspeople? Is there any kind of heuristic process that would enable the senior management team to predict an event of such magnitude, allowing it to prepare the organization for a recession?

The answer is at once both ominous and enlightening. On the one hand, it is very difficult to predict the moment at which a recession will occur and to accurately estimate its magnitude. On the other hand, there are simple indicators that suggest when something is awry and when the risk of a recession is high. These signals usually take the form of economic imbalances, which function like a rubber band: the farther they are stretched in one direction, the greater the force with which they will snap back in the other direction.

Typically, severe recessions result from one of, or a combination of, three sources: external credit shocks, stock market bubbles, and real estate bubbles.

Recessions generated by an external credit shock can be caused by factors that are exclusively local or can also come from the outside world in general. In both cases, a change in the movement of global capital flows will affect a national economy only if the economy is facing great difficulty in renewing its debt obligations. This usually suggests that the country has a large fiscal deficit and a high level of debt in comparison with its gross domestic product (GDP). This is well illustrated by examples from Latin America and Asia during the 1990s and from central and eastern Europe during the 2000s.

What is the debt level at which a country falls into serious risk? Regrettably, the answer is that "it depends." European countries can continue to grow economically even when their debt-to-GDP levels exceed 100 percent. In contrast, Latin American countries face significant risk when their debt-to-GDP levels surpass 70 percent. The general rule is that the higher the degree of institutional instability, the lower the level of debt that places a country at risk of facing a severe recession.

The probability of a recession as a result of a stock market bubble usually relates directly to the level of capitalization of the economy. In countries with a lower level of capitalization, recessions that arise from stock market bubbles are much less common.

Finally, there are recessions caused by real estate bubbles. The indiscriminate granting of mortgage credits is a sign that the country is facing a rising risk of recession, as happened in the United States in the lead-up to the financial crisis that started in 2007. There sometimes is an external factor that acts as the final trigger for this type of recession, such as a decrease in the prices of raw materials in a country dependent on primary resources, or perhaps a chain or series of bankruptcies that negatively affects mortgage loans.

In a study of twenty-one OECD countries during the period 1960–2007, Stijn Claessens, Ayhan Kose, and Marco Terrones detected seventy-six recessions and identified 122 different causes. The authors group the underlying causes into the following categories: ten were credit crunches, thirty-one were stock market bubbles, eighteen were exclusively from a real estate bubble, and the remainder resulted from a combination of these factors.

The year 2007 was witness to the worst global recession since 1928. While there has been a period of growth since the financial crisis at the end of the first decade of the twenty-first century, many Western economies have slowed considerable, while some have experienced additional recessions. Greece, for example, was in recession for sixty-three consecutive months between the third quarter of 2008 and the second quarter of 2014, while productivity per person in Italy was at a lower level in 2015 than it had been in 2007. On the other side of the world, between the first quarter of 2012 and the second quarter of 2015, Japan experienced negative GDP growth in six of fourteen quarters.

Drawing on what we explored in chapter 6, the probability of an economy's entrance into a severe recession augments a company's need to increase its strategic flexibility. In general, flexibility implies assuming costs that give rise to a certain tension with other short-term objectives.

DIAGNOSING AND MOBILIZING THE ORGANIZATION WHEN FACED WITH CONCURRENT CHALLENGES

The challenges faced by the senior management team are multidimensional and do not surface in isolation from one another. The ability to prioritize how to address them is of a fundamental importance. It is not possible to fight battles on all fronts at once given the energy that each of these requires. A fundamental part of strategic leadership is identifying and acting on the most pressing matters to ensure the survival and healthy growth of the organization.

Identifying the presence of a single strategic leadership challenge is relatively simple given that it is accompanied by changes in the environmental context that are identifiable with significant precision. What is more complex is prioritizing between challenges when more than one is present.

One of the first steps is to determine what kind of challenges you are dealing with. Are they developmental? Creative? The competitive process dominates and gives order and meaning to the other processes. The emergency challenge always has a contingent effect on the future of the industry and the organization's priorities. Overall, industry-wide forces and changes are more dominant than macroeconomic changes. The developmental challenge, therefore, takes precedence over the emergency challenge. Organizational development problems have a degree of independence from strategic management challenges but cannot be analyzed clearly unless the organization first identifies the type of strategic leadership challenges it faces.

In terms of minimizing organizational pain, the best time to take on an organizational design issue is when a company is not going through an adaptive strategic challenge. The senior management team must constantly take into consideration the organization's size and age in its decision-making, instituting changes where appropriate to survival and growth.

USING INFORMAL AUTHORITY TO MOBILIZE ACTION WHEN FACING CONCURRENT CHALLENGES

We worked with the minority partner of a regional professional services company in Montevideo, Uruguay, that faced a complex challenge. Its formal organizational design was no longer sufficient for the size of the organization. In addition, changes in the external competitive context triggered a surge in demand for the company's products. It was then that its organizational deficiencies became more pronounced, but the majority partner simply did not appear to react to the difficulties that arose as a result. He was reluctant to establish a formal system that allowed younger employees to become partners in the future.

What made things especially difficult was that the minority partner needed to mobilize organizational change, but he did not appreciate the formal authority required to do so. While he did have some authority, it was the majority partner who had the absolute prerogative to initiate or halt any change to the organization's formal design. Moreover, only the majority partner had the power to make changes in the ownership structure. As a result, the minority partner needed to undertake a mobilizing intervention fraught with risk. No one else seemed capable of mounting a response sufficient to meet the dual challenge facing the company. That is, making adjustments to formal organizational design and responding to the acceleration in demand.

The above case is useful for addressing a few guidelines for designing interventions. The first point has to do with the amount of learning that is necessary. The more internal processes that are grappling with changes, the greater the level of systemic learning is required. Making adaptive learning interventions often lead to lots of frustration. Authority figures are the first to encounter this organizational frustration, as everyone expects them to resolve conflicts, sparing them the pain of loss, in whatever form that may take. Any authority figure who is unconvinced of change will find it difficult to endure and sustain these waves of frustration, guiding their colleagues toward learning. Only those who understand the need and internalize the purpose will take on their share of the adaptive work. Therefore, individuals leading change processes must exercise extreme caution in order to avoid rupturing the system and making themselves convenient scapegoats for stakeholders who would prefer not to deal with the problem.

Although a system can be mobilized toward change without relying on an organization's formal authority, if not enough attention is paid to that formal authority, the probability of success decreases enormously. In professional service firms, where formal authority and property overlap, the need for formal authority engagement is highest. Unlike anyone else, formal authority figures can establish the holding environments that are necessary for learning and change. The greater the systemic learning required, the greater the need for such holding environments. It follows, therefore, that both formal authority figures and the holding environment they create are necessary when addressing an adaptive strategic challenge and vital when an organization is confronted by two or more concurrent adaptive strategic challenges.

As such, in the face of concurrent challenges, it is advisable that the initial intervention involves the formal authority. Once formal authorities are on board, the success of interventions planned to affect the organization in general is much more likely.

Again, no matter how many challenges the company is dealing with at the same time, we recommend designing interventions that always begin with an assessment of the external environment. First, this needs to take into consideration the immediate competitive environment, then the macroeconomic environment, and, finally, the inner dynamics that emerge from organizational design. Guidance for each of these steps has been provided in summary form in the preceding pages at the end of our analysis of each leadership challenge.

CHAPTER 11

THE FUTURE OF STRATEGY AS LEADERSHIP

The fundamental hidden assumption of the four strategic leadership challenges is that the evolution of the business environment obeys general laws. It follows, therefore, that it is more than likely that they will repeat in the future. Because of these laws, we can focus on what can be predicted about future changes. This will help companies both prepare for their navigation and facilitate organizational sensemaking when they inevitably find themselves caught up in these changes.

Today, the world is experiencing unprecedented change. The fourth industrial revolution is a concept that summarizes the technological innovation of the past few decades. Already, this has had a dramatic impact on how we live and on how our organizations add value to society. These changes have occurred globally, resulting in a new type of consumer as well as new business models. The concepts of the gig economy and platform organizations, for example, have served to dismantle traditional notions about the boundaries between corporations, business partners, suppliers, and customers. They put into question how, where, when, and with whom we work.

Another consequence has been the emergence of companies of unprecedented scale. Some now surpass nation-states in terms of the number of people involved, their reach, economy, and influence. By 2018, for example, the number of Facebook users was almost one-third of the global population. By February 2020, Microsoft, Apple, Amazon, and Alphabet were the four largest companies in the United States, measured in terms of market capitalization, each with a value of over one trillion dollars. Only fourteen countries have higher GDPs.

This new world is generating different social tensions, with an increase in income inequality in most developed countries over the past forty years as well as a burgeoning awareness of and concern about the environmental effects of unchecked consumerism, exploitation of natural resources, and emissions.

In this new context, is it reasonable to sustain our assumption of laws that refer to a repetitive evolutionary process? To what extent do these changes generate a degree of novelty that could lead to different social processes and strategic leadership challenges? If adjustments to the processes outlined in this book are necessary, how marginal or extensive should they be?

The objective of this final chapter is to address the future, allowing for new perspectives on the four strategic leadership challenges on which we have focused in the previous chapters. First, we describe some of the fundamental changes the world is facing. Next, we analyze their effect on the four challenges. In short, our expectation is that the four challenges will continue to be at the center of business activity for the foreseeable future.

GLOBAL TRENDS

Since the advent of the industrial age in the eighteenth century, which ushered in the use of the steam engine and mechanical production, we have witnessed an acceleration in technological innovation and its impact on how we work and where we live as well as on our methods of transportation, communication, and organization. Klaus Schwab, the founder of the World Economic Forum, argues that we have experienced four distinct phases of industrial revolution.[1] If the first was based on steam and mechanization, then the second was dependent on electricity and assembly lines, while the third had its foundations in computing and the emergence of digital platforms and services.

The fourth industrial revolution has leveraged the opportunities made possible by the third. The connection and combination of different digital technologies has placed an emphasis on sharing and interoperation. The internet facilitates the accumulation of big data. Every two years, the world collects as much data as it gathered in all the previous years. From big data it is a short step, via statistics and algorithms, to artificial intelligence (AI). The possibility to train systems to learn automatically unleashes tremendous forces with the potential to address global challenges. Meanwhile, information and communication technologies facilitate the emergence of the internet of things, with the possibility of controlling artifacts at a distance and with significant degrees of precision. These technologies open up new prospects in terms of learning and education (e.g., MOOCS—massive open online courses), detecting and finding cures for disease through AI, and even solving the problem of cheap housing with the use of 3D printing.

One salient change these technologies enable is the emergence of the global, connected, digital consumer.[2] The prevalence of social media during the current century has transformed how many people live, accounting for around one-seventh of an individual's working life. Much of people's time is now spent in work, with their families, and making use of social media platforms—in that order. Social media, then, is displacing many other activities.

Such consumer behavior is dramatically changing businesses. According to Statista, in March 2020, nearly 63 percent of global internet users preferred to start their searches on Amazon, 44 percent on Google, and only 21 percent on website of the brand they want. It is not surprising, therefore, that brand awareness has substantially reduced over the last decade, with the increase in the importance of Amazon and Google as sources of information.

Another consequence of the technological revolution and changes in consumer behavior has been the increased speed of business scalability. For instance, it took 25.8 years for Microsoft to reach one billion Windows users, whereas WhatsApp required only 6.8 years to achieve the same figure.

Behavioral and technological changes also have enabled the gig economy, a free market system where organizations and independent workers engage in short-term work arrangements. According to the US Bureau of Labor Statistics (BLS), the US gig economy had fifty-five million participants in 2017. It is estimated that 36 percent of US workers take part in the gig economy, and 33 percent of companies, including the likes of Uber and Airbnb, make extensive use of gig workers.

An important characteristic of these gig-dependent industries is the platform structure. Uber, for instance, consists of a system were drivers participate. Uber competes against other platforms, trying to attract drivers and customers to its service. The platform structure will necessarily lead to a certain degree of industry consolidation, as we discussed in chapter 3. Traditional competitors—such as established taxi companies—have been confronted by a creative challenge, as discussed in chapter 4, with the rise of Uber and similar platform organizations. How will the different challenges now manifest themselves in this changed industry? Will they be any different from the patterns we have outlined earlier in this book?

SOME UNEXPECTED AND UNWANTED RESULTS

The first consequence of the combination of new technologies and global customers is the dominance of a few large, global technology companies. As of November 2020, the five largest companies in the United States, measured in terms of market capitalization, were Apple Inc. ($B2024), Microsoft ($B1618), Amazon Inc. ($B1590), Alphabet Inc. ($B1191), and Facebook Inc. ($B789).[3] Tesla, which many also consider a technology company that blurs the boundaries with car manufacturing and the clean energy industry, stands in sixth place on this list.

All of these five technology giants have significant levels of globalization. In 2019, their non-US revenues ranged between 30 percent and almost 70 percent of the total revenues.

The economic might and global reach of these organizations outstrips several nation-states. In a somewhat artificial comparison, we find that sales revenues of many global corporations outstrip the GDP of a huge number of countries. At the time of writing, for example, Apple's market capitalization was on a par with the GDP of both Australia and Spain, while exceeding that of Mexico, Indonesia, The Netherlands, Saudi Arabia, Turkey, and Switzerland.[4]

The wealth of corporations and nations is also evidenced by comparing corporate cash availability and national central bank reserves. Both are proxy of the power to affect asset values. In that case, Apple's total cash and short-term investments in September 2019 was U$B100.5,[5] while the Brazilian central bank reserves (the tenth largest worldwide) was U$B379.4 by the end of 2018.[6]

Size and market power partially explain the emergence of global oligopolies. Meanwhile, the creation and destruction of companies has decreased. The US census reports that the rate of company creation decreased from 13 percent in the early 1980s to 8 percent in 2016 while company closures reduced from around 10 percent to 8 percent in the same period. These figures might indicate a decrease in the underlying forces behind the process of "creative destruction" described in chapters 1 to 4.

Unsurprisingly, the productivity of the economy is also falling in the Organization for Economic Cooperation and Development (OECD) countries. US productivity experienced annual increases of 1.5 percent to 2.5 percent in the 1950s and 1960s but has dropped below 1 percent in recent decades. Similar figures from other OECD countries like the United Kingdom, France, Mexico, and Chile confirm the decrease in creative destruction.

Union membership has declined for decades, and with it the level of union-related intervention in corporate affairs. In 1985, 30 percent of workers in OECD countries were labor union members; in 2017 only 17 percent. The gig economy has had a particular effect on labor union participation. New gig-related business models make it more difficult for unions to provide coordination and value. OECD studies also indicate that productivity is growing faster than minimum and average salaries.[7] Meanwhile, levels of inequality have increased since the 1980s in the United States and most European countries.

INCREASING ENVIRONMENTAL CONCERNS

The third and fourth industrial revolutions resulted in unprecedented gains in many of the indicators that we use to gauge progress in human development, from life expectancy to per capita income to education. However, this happened at a cost in air and water pollution, the loss of tropical forests, and the build-up of greenhouse gases in the atmosphere.

Consumption of natural resources by modern industrial economies remains very high—in the range of 45 to 85 metric tons per person annually when all factors are counted, including soil erosion, mining wastes, and other ancillary materials. It currently requires about 300 kilograms of natural resources to generate $100 of income in the world's most advanced economies. This volume of material represents environmental alteration on a truly massive scale.[8]

Recently, risks analysts have promoted the notion of climate-change-related "green swan" events—that is, disruptive environmental events that could be behind the next systemic financial crisis, triggering complex and unpredictable chain reactions. In this vein, the global recession triggered by the spread of COVID-19 is a sad and related example. In the context of our book, a green swan event reinforces the validity of the emergency challenge.

Large companies are setting sustainability goals to mitigate these problems. For instance, Repsol, a global oil company based in Spain, recently became the first large oil and gas company to set a goal of becoming carbon neutral by 2050. Meanwhile, Microsoft recently announced an ambitious goal to become carbon negative by 2030, without the use of offsets.

In spite of such initiatives, highly valued as they are, the environmental problems will not be resolved by individuals or organizations acting alone. The planet has reached a point of resource saturation, and the consequences are likely to be highly unpredictable for all who inhabit it.

CHANGES IN THE FINANCIAL REGULATORY SYSTEM

Changes in global regulations and financial systems provide more factors to consider in assessing the emergency challenge. In 1980, the US Congress passed the Depository Institutions Deregulation and Monetary Control Act, which served to deregulate financial institutions that accept deposits while strengthening the Federal Reserve's control over monetary policy. All of this deregulation helped accelerate a trend toward increasing banking organizations' complexity as they moved to more significant consolidation and conglomeration. Financial institution mergers increased with the total number of banking organizations consolidating to under 8,000 in 2008 from a previous peak of nearly 15,000 in the early 1980s. While banks have grown, the conglomeration of different financial services under one organization has also increased the complexity of those services. Banks began offering new financial products like derivatives and began packaging traditional financial assets like mortgages together through securitization.

Since the Great Recession of 2007–9, the United States has regulated the financial system through the Dodd-Frank Wall Street Reform and Consumer Protection Act. This law includes eight components to help prevent a repeat of the 2008 financial crisis. However, concerns about the financial system's future stability remain. The reasons relate to some of the measures the rest of the world took to alleviate the consequences of the Great Recession. An example of these measures is the programs of mass bond-buying by central banks to stimulate the global economy. Interestingly, these measures affect not only the United States but also most of the developed world.

From the European Central Bank to the Federal Reserve, central banks made large-scale purchases of corporate bonds and other financial assets after the Great Recession to stimulate economic recovery and raise inflation toward its targeted level. These corporate bonds carried an appreciable risk of default, but their yield was barely enough to cover inflation. Consequently, credit risk wasn't priced in at all.[9] The consequence is that the central banks' balance sheets are weaker, and the global economy faces greater volatility.

FOR THE SAKE OF A NEW GLOBAL ORDER

We are entering an era of higher financial turbulence, larger oligopolies, weaker unions, and considerable social discontent. The effect of human activity on the natural environment demands substantial changes in our production and consumption patterns.

The global discussion has to shift toward the need for regulation and coordination at a planetary level. The solution to future challenges is far from trivial. It will require that we rethink and remodel global institutions concerned with trade, finance, and environmental control. The gig economy, for example, will demand new regulatory patterns and a different approach to social security systems.

The path to new institutional rule is never smooth, nor does it extend in a straight line between two points. Instead, it resembles a sinuous process of advancements and regressions. Processes of institutional reconfiguration are among the most turbulent ones. In this context, it is fair to question whether the strategic leadership challenges this book describes will remain essential. Do they have future validity?

THE FUTURE OF THE DEVELOPMENTAL AND CREATIVE CHALLENGES

We think that the four strategic leadership challenges will continue to occupy a central role in the agenda of senior management teams over the coming decades. We will explain the motives and consider some necessary adjustments to these challenges. To start with, we need to take into account the effect of recent global trends on the evolutionary mechanisms that inform and shape the strategic challenges.

The technological revolution opened up multiple business opportunities, generating the creation of new industries and, consequently, new processes of creative destruction. However, the evolution of these industries may have deviated from what we have become accustomed to over previous decades. We need to consider the degree of consolidation in these new industries. For instance, how many companies will remain in the TV streaming sector? What is going to happen in online marketplaces? Or in car sharing?

In maturing industries, the creative challenge is a visible threat, and it is reasonable to expect that this will repeat in the future. As such, taxi companies in emerging markets will face the creative challenge as car-sharing systems become global.

However, when considering the validity of the challenges in the future, the question that matters relates to those that are now generating the creative challenge. Will Amazon face the creative challenge? Will Google face disruption?

The answer, of course, is yes. Although, given the decrease in industry turnarounds, we expect a delay of any disruption that is likely to threaten Amazon's competitive position.

The paradox is that, although we observe an acceleration in the appearance of new technologies, we do not necessarily see an increase in the emergence of creative challenges in the future.

Is the developmental challenge likely to be encountered in the near future? As all new industries have a limit to their growth potential, we expect that all companies within any of these industries will face the developmental challenge. That is, even Amazon, in the web service business, Facebook, and Google will be confronted by it one day. It is just a matter of time before many of their business units will experience much lower rates of growth and the problems that arise from market saturation. However, as these huge organizations have monopolistic power, the transition to maturity might be less dramatic than that for a company facing multiple competitors.

THE FUTURE OF THE EMERGENCY CHALLENGE

The world is becoming more unstable. The balance sheets of central banks look worse than before the 2007–9 global crisis. Corporate leverage ratios too. As productivity decreases, companies push their leverage ratio to sustain sales growth.

Meanwhile, global commercial agreements are being thrown into question. The full effects of Brexit and the replacement of the North American Free Trade Agreement (NAFTA) with the United States–Mexico–Canada Agreement (USMCA) are yet to be fully appreciated. The aftershocks will be experienced for years to come both in trading and diplomatic relationships. Global coordination as we know it today will look very different in the future. There will be less integration between countries, greater isolation, and more macroeconomic volatility. In general, there is likely to be a shift of emphasis from the global to the local.

An imminent widespread recession is increasingly likely. The COVID-19 crisis is an example of an unexpected event that rapidly triggers such recessions, highlighting the global difficulties of easing their effects. This crisis is going to test the capacity of both central banks and the welfare state. People in the gig economy are already suffering, losing their clients, and finding themselves unable to deliver work. Multiple organizations will fold, and numerous people will have to declare bankruptcy. Besides, we will observe an increase in insurance claims by those forced by governments to close their businesses or unable to travel. The emergency challenge has become even more significant and essential than was the case in the past.

THE FUTURE OF THE STRUCTURAL CHALLENGE

In a world with stronger global oligopolies and lower productivity, everything points toward the start of a downward supercycle. Recent estimates indicate that the downward phase of the supercycle started in 2014 and should continue well into the future. The specific length of the downturn will depend on the duration of the pandemic-driven weakness in global demand and the steps taken to mitigate climate change.[10] In a world of higher macroeconomic volatility, we would expect more variations in the short and medium terms' commodity cycles.

Companies will face the structural challenge. It could be alleviated by the emergence of a big nation growing very fast. China is not in a condition to continue growing at the same rate as in the past, but India might replace China. Until then, commodity prices are more likely to face long-term reductions. The structural challenge will affect multiple commodity companies for the foreseeable future.

FINAL WORDS

We can take it for granted that leadership will continue to be tested for years to come. We will be challenged by the unexpected, as witness the outbreak, rapid spread, and health-related and economic devastation of COVID-19. The simultaneity, interdependence, and combination of such challenges will add to the complexity of modern life.

We trust, however, that our exploration of the challenges in this book and our guidance on how they might be navigated can serve you well in the future. There still remains much to learn about their ongoing evolution and the implications of change. As such, we would like to invite readers to share their stories and experiences with us. In this way, we can carry on learning together and help guide tomorrow's leaders with new insights and recommendations.

Even as we find ourselves in the midst of a global pandemic, and can witness the effects of technological change, globalization, and social tension, we remain convinced that the strategic challenges will continue to repeat themselves in one form or another for the foreseeable future. We also will continue to observe enormous organizational pressures that arise from dealing with predictable changes. Indeed, it is this very predictability that underpins our conviction that *strategy is leadership*.

THE KEY CONCEPTS OF ADAPTIVE LEADERSHIP

Our *Strategy as Leadership* approach uses different models to conceptualize the competitive environment's evolution and draws on adaptive leadership tools. The reader may have noticed that we emphasize the explanation of those processes that refer to the evolution of the competitive environment, choosing to avoid unnecessary repetition of adaptive leadership concepts, which have been well developed in several other texts.[1] This appendix aims to provide additional support on adaptive leadership for those unfamiliar with it, providing an essential tool kit for understanding the key concepts. While of interest to anyone who wishes to exercise strategic leadership, this appendix will be of particular utility to consultants and educators.[2]

TYPES OF PROBLEMS

Adaptive leadership addresses adaptive problems, which should be differentiated from technical problems. Strategic leadership problems are adaptive problems that, unfortunately, are often confused both in theory and in practice with technical problems.

For many challenges in people's lives, experts or authorities can solve their problems and meet their needs. They look to doctors to make them healthy, mechanics to fix their cars, accountants to organize their taxes, and bosses to resolve disputes. People give them power, authorizing them to find solutions, and often they can deliver. Problems that can be solved through the knowledge of experts or senior authorities are technical challenges. The fact that problems are technical does not imply that they are simple. Instead, it means that there are available and adequate solutions to these problems. For example, the need for heart surgery is not a simple matter but—because both the problem and the procedure for solving it are known—it is a technical problem.

By contrast, the problems that require leadership are those that the experts cannot solve. These are adaptive challenges. The solutions lie not in technical answers but, rather, in people themselves. The mechanic can fix the car brakes but cannot stop the driver from speeding. The surgeon can attend to the patient's heart condition, but she cannot change the patient's unhealthy habits. The same happens in organizations. All the leadership strategic challenges covered in this book are adaptive challenges that cannot be solved by authorities alone.

Adaptive leadership challenges see people as part of the problem, requiring their engagement and their development of new capabilities. The formal authority alone cannot provide the solution. But it has the responsibility for setting the conditions for gathering all the "necessary actors" together to make sense of the adaptive challenge as well as sustaining the creative and conflicting process of resolution.

Finding the way will be an arduous challenge because the acquisition of the new capacities necessary to solve the problem will require deep learning. This, in turn, requires that individual, group, divisional, and organizational habits, beliefs, and values are audited and questioned. In other words, adaptive problems are those problems whose solution requires dealing with the conflicts in the underlying values held by different stakeholders as they pertain to the problem at hand.

Identifying the type of problem an organization faces is often tricky. For instance, coronary bypass surgeries frequently do involve adaptive problems, because heart problems can result from bad habits and mistaken beliefs. The solution involves not only surgery and the skill of a technician but also the adaptation of behavior, requiring action by the patient, their family, and friends. Close to 500,000 coronary bypass surgeries are performed every year in the United States alone. However, with the substantial alteration of population habits, this number could drop dramatically.

In business, the challenges similarly combine technical and adaptive problems, making it essential to distinguish between the two and gain holistic understanding. If, say, a machine's temperature becomes too high during a chemical process, a technician or engineer is required to address the problem. But behind this technical problem, there may be an adaptive problem relating to the need to increase the machine's workload because its output is not satisfying the level of demand. Further, behind this problem of unsatisfied demand, there may be a coordination problem between production, logistics, and sales, stemming from a change in the circumstances of the business's customers. Accordingly, what can, in the first instance, be seen as a technical problem with an easy solution (an overheating machine) is revealed, at the core, to be a problem requiring the development of new organizational capacities and systemic learning by the entire company.

AUTHORITY AND LEADERSHIP

Having identified the type of problem, we now shift to another compelling distinction: that between authority and leadership. Ronald Heifetz and Marty Linsky highlight that most people tend to presume that a leader is a person in a formal authority position—the boss, the CEO, the president, the captain, the expert. However, exercising leadership is different from holding a high position in an organizational hierarchy, and different from authoritative expertise. It is also different from having enormous informal power derived from credibility, trust, respect, admiration, or moral authority. There are numerous examples of people in positions of senior authority (as well as people reluctant to risk losing their informal power) who have never led their organizations through difficult but necessary adaptive change.

Adaptive leadership understands authority—whether formal or informal—as the power entrusted by one party to another in exchange for a service. The basic services, or social functions, authorities provide are (1) direction, (2) protection, and (3) order. As in nature, all organizations depend on such roles and their functions to maintain equilibrium within the social system. However, these functions, although useful, are markedly insufficient in the practice of leadership.

Leadership, from this perspective, is the practice of mobilizing people—groups, organizations, societies—to address their most challenging problems. Effective leadership addresses problems that require people to move from a familiar but inadequate equilibrium—through disequilibrium—to a more adequate equilibrium. Acts of leadership assist people in moving beyond the edge of familiar patterns into the unknown terrain of greater complexity, new learning, and new behaviors, usually requiring loss, grief, conflict, risk, stress, and creativity. Often, deeply held values are both at stake and under review. Seen in this light, authority becomes only one resource—and sometimes a constraint—in the practice of leadership. To lead, often a person must act beyond his or her level of authorization. It is because of this that leadership is risky. The dangers reside in the need to challenge the expectations of the very people who grant the formal and informal authority.

All the strategic adaptive challenges described in this book demand costly adjustments that involve learning new ways of work, letting go of valuable benefits, renegotiating some loyalties, and taking responsibility beyond what people expect to do or are used to handling. Consequently, all too frequently, people are reluctant to authorize leadership. Instead, they authorize protection. They are willing to allow authorities to solve their difficult problems but are unwilling to face the painful trade-offs required. Therefore, people in power usually receive mixed messages. They are asked to solve problems but to protect their colleagues from the losses that result from change.

SYSTEMS, FACTIONS, AND INDIVIDUALS

In nature, everything is related to everything else. The same applies in organizations, which are complex entanglements of relationships. A common problem for the exercise of leadership is to look at organizations in terms of mechanical, isolated parts instead of as organic, living social systems. Adaptive leadership scholars define a social system as any collective enterprise—small group, organization, network of organizations, nation, the world—with shared challenges that has interdependent and, therefore, interactive dynamics and features.

The nature of an adaptive challenge is that it is systemic. The first step in tackling any adaptive challenge, therefore, is to diagnose the system. The diagnostic work involves gaining perspective on organizational culture, observing patterns of behaviors, understanding networks of relationships, and identifying default responses to adaptive problems. It is necessary to look at the big picture, to understand its complexity, and to identify how the system congregates in factions around the adaptive challenge.

A faction, within the system, is a group with a shared perspective that has been shaped by tradition, power relationships, loyalties, and interests. It has its own internal logic to understand the adaptive challenge and make sense of its resolution. Systemic analysis is enabled by effective mapping of factions, something that depicts the groups relevant to an adaptive challenge, and includes the loyalties, values, and losses at risk that keep each faction invested in its position.

The composition of factions is not rigid or stable over time. Instead, factions evolve. It is the objective of leadership to help them evolve, and converse with each other so that they can better solve the adaptive challenges. Moreover, one individual can participate simultaneously in several factions—since the definition of the faction changes with the definition of the problem.

ADAPTIVE WORK AND THE CHANGES IN THE COMPETITIVE ENVIRONMENT

To exercise leadership is to mobilize adaptive work and help systems thrive.[3] Adaptive work consists of holding people in a sustained period of disequilibrium during which they identify what cultural DNA to conserve, what to discard, what to invent, and what to discover in order to enable them to thrive in the face of challenge.

Although they cannot alone solve the adaptive challenges, senior management teams are responsible for setting the conditions that enable identification of the challenges and help the system anticipate and carry out the adaptive work. This book is intended to assist this process.

Table A.1 describes the four strategic leadership challenges covered in the book as well as their distinguishing features. All of these challenges are of a magnitude sufficient to compromise the organization's future. However, the particular dynamics and risks associated with each are different.

Correctly identifying the type of cycle and, above all, the kind of leadership challenge is essential for determining the organization's priorities. In three of the strategic leadership challenges, organizations need to moderately upgrade their competencies (several of the organization's current competencies will remain useful in future competitive environments). In the creative challenge, however, the adjustment is significant as a large proportion of organizational competencies will become obsolete and will have to be replaced by new ones. Consequently, the change in the organizational cultural DNA will also be significant.

Some transitions demand permanent adjustments in organizational competencies while others require only temporary adjustments. However, even in these cases, companies will need to develop long-lasting capabilities to successfully address these temporary changes.

The adaptive work is more uncertain in some challenges than others. For example, in the developmental challenge, as in the emergency challenge, there is more clarity about the destination, about what the industry will look like, and what its strategic priorities will be. Conversely, in the structural challenge, the uncertainty is more significant. The creative challenge is undoubtedly the most uncertain of all.

HOLDING ENVIRONMENT AND PRODUCTIVE TENSION

Adaptive work requires two conditions for progress: holding environments and productive tension. Both need each other for learning and adaptation to occur. Without holding environments, tension is either avoided or becomes so high that it becomes unproductive.

Holding environments refer to the cohesive properties of a relationship or social system that serve to keep people engaged with one another despite the divisive forces generated by adaptive work. They may include,

TABLE A.1. Typology of strategic leadership challenges

Type of transitional competitive setting	Level of competency adjustment	Duration of new competencies required	Degree of certainty
Developmental challenge Transition from developing industry to mature industry	Moderate	Permanent	Relatively certain
Creative challenge Establishment of a new industry	Significant	Permanent	Highly uncertain
Emergency challenge Macroeconomic recession	Moderate	Temporary	Relatively certain
Structural challenge Downturn of the commodity cycle	Moderate	Semipermanent	Relatively uncertain

for example, bonds of affiliation and love; agreed-on rules, procedures, and norms; shared purposes and common values; traditions, language, and rituals; familiarity with adaptive work; and trust in authority. Holding environments give a group identity and contain the conflict, chaos, and confusion often produced when struggling with complex problematic realities.

In strategic adaptive challenges, as in all adaptive challenges, organizational authorities have privileged resources to establish holding environments. In this book, we propose that they can use the strategic planning process as a safe setting to shed light on the challenges, help these challenges ripen within the different factions, and orchestrate conflicting conversations. The establishment of an experimental business unit could be another example of a holding environment. The conviction of the authority to sustain the organization's search for a solution is another example.

Together with establishing the holding environment, the exercise of leadership requires productive tension. Productive tension is the level of stress that allows the system to learn. Systemic and individual learning and transformation require people to navigate through a period of disequilibrium and disturbance. This disequilibrium emerges from conflict, frustration, confusion, disorientation, and fear of losing something dear.

The purpose of leadership is to make progress on a tough collective challenge, not to elevate productive tension per se. However, without an adequate level of tension, progress will not be achieved. If tension is too low, it is because the system has not addressed the issues and is consciously or unconsciously sustaining the status quo. If the tension is too high, however, the system can be seriously harmed, as factions fight and become more polarized rather than learning together. In this scenario, the real adaptive issues remain unaddressed.

NOTES

INTRODUCTION

1. We are indebted to several scholars for the theoretical foundations that underpin our study. From the evolutionary economics perspective, we owe a debt to the lifelong research of Steven Klepper. The Austrian economist Joseph Schumpeter has inspired our understanding of strategic management thinking. Ronald Heifetz and Marty Linsky, of the John F. Kennedy School of Government at Harvard University, provided us with the theoretical framework of adaptive leadership. Dean Williams, with his categorization of leadership challenges in *Real Leadership*, inspired us to connect adaptive leadership with particular environmental changes. Finally, our colleague Rodolfo Rivarola has contributed significantly to our thinking about the relationship between strategic priorities and group losses.

CHAPTER 1: THE DEVELOPMENTAL CHALLENGE

1. "Global Smartphone Shipments from 2009 to 2020," Statista, accessed December 3, 2020, https://www.statista.com/.

2. The book was translated into English in 1934.

3. "Global Smartphone Shipments from 2009 to 2020."

4. These statistics summarize results from the twentieth century reported in Steve

Klepper and Elizabeth Graddy, "The Evolution of New Industries and the Determinants of Market Structure," *RAND Journal of Economics* 21, no. 1 (Spring 1990): 27–44.

5. "Long-Term Price Trends for Computers, TVs, and Related Items," US Bureau of Labor Statistics, accessed December 18, 2020, https://www.bls.gov/.

6. Klepper and Graddy "Evolution of New Industries and the Determinants of Market Structure," 27–44.

CHAPTER 2: NAVIGATING THE DEVELOPMENTAL CHALLENGE

1. The reader will recognize similarities between the challenges that we have identified and what Dean Williams explores in *Real Leadership: Helping People and Organizations Face Their Toughest Challenges* (San Francisco: Berrett-Koehler, 2005). Indeed, we are indebted to Williams for inspiring us. However, it is worth noting that there are fundamental differences between the two approaches. Where Williams is concerned with identifying general leadership challenges, we are focused on particular environmental changes and the challenges they generate.

2. Ronald Heifetz, Alexander Grashow, and Marty Linsky, *The Practice of Adaptive Leadership: Tools and Tactics for Changing Your Organization and the World* (Boston: Harvard Business Press, 2009).

CHAPTER 3: PREPARING FOR THE DEVELOPMENTAL CHALLENGE

1. "Apple Moves from #5 to #4 in Global Laptop Shipments, on Track for Double-Digit Share," 9TO5.Mac, accessed December 3, 2020, https://9to5mac.com/2018/02/12/apple-mac-market-share/.https://9to5mac.com/2018/02/12/apple-mac-market-share/

2. Richard Post Rumelt, "Towards a Strategic Theory of the Firm," in *Competitive Strategic Management*, ed. Robert Lamb (Englewood Cliffs, NJ: Prentice-Hall, 1984), 556–70.

3. Dennis Cary Mueller, "First-Mover Advantages and Path Dependence," *International Journal of Industrial Organization* 15, no. 6 (1997): 827–50.

4. The Zona Austral division included Argentina and Chile.

CHAPTER 4: THE CREATIVE CHALLENGE

1. Barnaby Feder, "Kodak's Quest for a New Camera," *New York Times*, December 6, 1981, accessed December 3, 2020, www.nytimes.com/1981/12/06/business/kodak-s-quest-for-a-new-camera.html.

2. "Small Business Failure Statistics to Know in 2020—A Realistic Picture," Fortunly, accessed December 3, 2020, https://fortunly.com/statistics/small-business-failure-statistics/#gref.

3. Scott Shane has compiled data on new business survival rates discriminated by industrial segment: "Small Business Failure Rates by Industry: The Real Numbers," Small Business Trends, last updated March 20, 2020, http://smallbiztrends.

com/. Shane makes use of information drawn from the US Pool on Competitive Dynamics from US Census.

4. Clayton Magleby Christensen, *The Innovator's Dilemma: When New Technologies Cause Great Firms to Fail* (Boston: Harvard Business Review Press, 2013).

5. "Le seul véritable voyage, le seul bain de Jouvence, ce ne serait pas d'aller vers de nouveaux paysages, mais d'avoir d'autres yeux, de voir l'univers avec les yeux d'un autre, de cent autres, de voir les cent univers que chacun d'eux voit, que chacun d'eux est." Marcel Proust, *Albertine Gone* (1925).

6. Roberto Vassolo and Guillermo N. Perkins, *La Nacion* (A), *IAE Business School Teaching Case* IAE-C111-01632-SP, 2005; Roberto Vassolo and Maricruz Barcia, *La Nación*, "Danone Aprende de una Crisis," *IAE Business School Teaching Case* IAE-C111-03036-SP, 2010.

7. "It's True: The Typical Car Is Parked 95 Percent of the Time," Streetsblog USA, accessed December 3, 2020, https://usa.streetsblog.org/.

CHAPTER 5: NAVIGATING THE CREATIVE CHALLENGE

1. Ronald Heifetz, Alexander Grashow, and Marty Linsky, *The Practice of Adaptive Leadership: Tools and Tactics for Changing Your Organization and the World* (Boston: Harvard Business Press, 2009).

2. William Brian Arthur, "Increasing Returns and the New World of Business," *Harvard Business Review* 74, no. 4 (April 1996): 100.

3. Karl Eduard Weick, *Sensemaking in Organizations* (Thousand Oaks, CA: Sage, 1995).

4. John Paul Kotter, "Accelerate!" *Harvard Business Review* 90, no. 11 (November 2012): 44–52.

5. Weick, *Sensemaking in Organizations*.

CHAPTER 6: THE EMERGENCY CHALLENGE

1. "What Happens after a Legendary CEO Departs?" PwC Network, accessed December 9, 2020, "www.strategyand.pwc.com/gx/en/insights/ceo-success.html.

2. "US Business Cycle Expansions and Contractions," National Bureau of Economic Research, accessed December 9, 2020, www.nber.org.

3. "Spanish aisles," *The Economist*, accessed December 3, 2020, http://www.economist.com/node/18775460

4. Fernando Fragueiro and Roberto Vassolo, "Danone Aprende de una Crisis," *IAE Business School Teaching Case* IAE-C111-02600-SP, 2009.

5. Rubén Figueiredo and Roberto Vassolo, "Arcos Dorados (A)," *IAE Business School Teaching Case* IAE-C112-03166-SP.

6. Stijn Claessens, Ayhan Kose, and Marco Terrones, "What Happens during Recessions, Crunches, and Busts?" *Economic Policy* 24, no. 60 (2008): 653–700.

7. Guillermo Calvo, Alejandro Izquierdo, and Ernesto Talvi, "Sudden Stops and Phoenix Miracles in Emerging Markets," *American Economic Review* 96, no. 2 (2006): 405–10.

8. Meghana Ayyagari, Asli Demirgüç-Kunt, and Vojislav Maksimovic, "Do Phoenix Miracles Exist? Firm-Level Evidence from Financial Crises," *World Bank Policy Research Working Paper Series*, vol. 1 (September 1, 2011).

9. This change has been defined as competitive leapfrogging. See Javier Garcia-Sanchez, Luiz Mesquita, and Roberto Santiago Vassolo, "What Doesn't Kill You Makes You Stronger: The Evolution of Competition and Entry-Order Advantages in Economically Turbulent Contexts," *Strategic Management Journal* 35, no. 13 (2014): 1972–92.

10. Roberto Vassolo, Tomás Reyes, Marco Sepulveda, and Joaquin Trucco, "Jump! The Effect of Recessions on Competitive Positioning," *Academy of Management Proceedings* 2017, no. 1 (2017): 13510.

11. "Top Vehicle Manufacturers in the US Market, 1961–2016," KNOEMA, accessed December 4, 2020, https://knoema.es/.

12. John A. Pearce II and Steven C. Michael, "Strategies to Prevent Economic Recessions from Causing Business Failure," *Business Horizons* 49 (2006): 201–09.

13. Adrián A. Cladart, "Crecimiento y diversificación de Martifer," *AESA Business School Teaching Case* DG-A-886(E)0-09-09-0119-1, 2009.

14. Pankaj Ghemawat, "The Risk of Not Investing in a Recession," *Sloan Management Review* (Spring 2009).

15. This is still an unpublished work carried out by Roberto Vassolo, Tomas Reyes, Consuelo Game, and Sergio Lazzarini.

16. The empirical evidence relating operating leverage to financial flexibility is still inconclusive. We base the argumentation on our results in the reported study.

CHAPTER 7: NAVIGATING THE EMERGENCY CHALLENGE

1. We observed this in the Danone case discussed in the previous chapter. For an extensive explanation of these types of commercial strategies, we recommend consulting Rafi Mohammed, "Ditch the Discounts," *Harvard Business Review* 89 (January–February 2011): 23–25.

2. In a recent study, Roberto Vassolo and colleagues analyzed the role of CEO overconfidence on firm-level performance during recessions. While the measure of overconfidence is indirect and does not capture what happens at the senior management team, the study supports the CEO's influence for creating a holding environment at the emergency challenge. The study is Tomás Reyes, Roberto Vassolo, Edgar Kausel, Diamela Torres, and Stephen Zhang, "Does Overconfidence Pay Off When Things Go Well? CEO Overconfidence, Firm Performance, and the Business Cycle," *Strategic Organization* (2020): 1476127020930659.

CHAPTER 8: THE STRUCTURAL CHALLENGE

1. We are aware that there is not total agreement in the use of the terms *cycle* and *supercycle*, and that what some people refer to as a supercycle, we call a cycle because of its shorter duration. This semantic difference is not a problem for understanding this chapter as long as the reader is conscious of the definitions we use.

2. Bilge Erten and José Antonio Ocampo, "The Future of Commodity Prices and the Pandemic-Driven Global Recession: Evidence from 150 Years of Data," *World Development* 137 (2021): 105164.

3. David Jacks, "From Boom to Bust: A Typology of Real Commodity Prices in the Long Run," *Cliometrica* 13, no. 2 (2019): 201–20.

4. Alfonso Cruz-Novoa, "Industrial Dynamics and Technological Structure of the Paper and Pulp Industry" (PhD diss., University of Sussex, 2011.)

5. Cruz-Novoa, "Industrial Dynamics and Technological Structure of the Paper and Pulp Industry." Cruz-Novoa created this figure, gathering information from the Beloit Paper Machine List containing the technological specifications of 968 machines manufactured by Beloit between 1862 and 1999. Beloit Corporation (previously Beloit Iron Works) was one of the leading manufacturers of paper technology in the world until it went bankrupt in 1999.

6. Alfonzo Cruz-Novoa, Tomás Reyes, and Robert Santiago Vassolo, "Liability of Middleness Revisited: The Advantages for Mid-Sized Competitors in Renewable Natural Resource Industries," *Management and Organization Review* 15, no. 4 (2019): 737–72.

7. Alfonzo Cruz-Novoa, Tomás Reyes, and Robert Santiago Vassolo, "Size Competition Revisited: The Advantages of Middle Size Competition in Commodity Industries," *Academy of Management Proceedings* 2016, no. 1 (2017): 10204.

8. As in every activity, there are other exceptions. For example, the production of lithium is growing at two-digit rates due to the demand for batteries for the storage of solar energy or providing energy to electric cars. However, even in these cases, fast growth rates last for a relatively short number of years until they stabilize.

9. Ramón Casadesus-Masanell, Jorge Tarzijan, and Jordan Mitchell, "Arauco (A): Forward Integration or Horizontal Expansion?" *Harvard Business School Teaching Case* 706S35-PDF-SPA, 2006.

10. Part of this chapter draws on a mathematical explanation outlined in Alejandro MacCawley, Angel Sevil, and Roberto Vassolo, "Entry-Timing Advantages in Renewable Natural Resources Industries," *Journal of Management Studies* 56, no. 7 (2019): 1482–512. This paper will be of interest to readers who wish to learn more about the theory of timing advantages and the commodity cycle.

11. A critical question regarding competition in natural resource industries relates to size. That is, the optimum organizational size for survival and for growth. There is a well-established school of thought that companies should either seek to

become large or remain small and occupy a niche position, because mid-sized organizations tend to face the most substantial market selection pressures. However, Cruz-Novoa, Reyes, and Vassolo ("Liability of Middleness Revisited") argue—and find empirical support for—the reverse. They claim that industries characterized by cost competition, the lack of product differentiation, large capital investments, and sharp price oscillation, favor mid-sized companies. Their study is essential to our thesis in this chapter, reinforcing the need to change strategic mental models. See also Roberto Vassolo, Ariel Casarin, and Sergio Lazzarini, "The Forgotten Competitive Arena: Strategy in Natural Resource Industries," *Academy of Management Perspectives* 34, no. 3 (2019): 378–99.

CHAPTER 10: LEADING THROUGH CONCURRENT CHALLENGES

1. Larry Greiner, "Evolution and Revolution as Organizations Grow," *Harvard Business Review* 76, no. 3 (March 1998): 55–64.

2. This claim is open to disagreement, as observed in Shane Oliver, "Has Australia Really Had Three Recessions in the last 28 Years?" Livewire, accessed December 4, 2020, www.livewiremarkets.com/.

CHAPTER 11: THE FUTURE OF STRATEGY AS LEADERSHIP

1. Klaus Schwab, *The Fourth Industrial Revolution* (New York: Crown Business, 2017).

2. Several of the following numbers and concepts were inspired in Scott Galloway, *The Four: The Hidden DNA of Amazon, Apple, Facebook, and Google* (New York: Random House, 2017).

3. "U.S. Commerce—Stock Market Capitalization of the 50 Largest American Companies," Weblists, updated November 30, 2020, www.iweblists.com/us/commerce/MarketCapitalization.html.

4. "At $1.3 Trillion, Apple Is Bigger Than These Things," Investopedia, accessed December 4, 2020, www.investopedia.com/news.

5. "Apple Inc.," Yahoo! Finance, accessed February 26, 2020, https://finance.yahoo.com/quote/AAPL/balance-sheet/.

6. "Brazil Total Reserves," World Bank Open Data, accessed February 26, 2020, https://data.worldbank.org/indicator/FI.RES.TOTL.CD.

7. "Decoupling of Wages from Productivity: What Implications for Public Policies?" *OECD Economic Outlook* 2018, no. 2 (2018).

8. "Global Trends," Sustainable Development Information Service, accessed December 4, 2020, www.griequity.com/resources/Environment/Global%20Environmental%20Trends.htm.

9. "The ECB's Bond-Buying Program Could Have Masked Major Risks," Business Insider, accessed February 26, 2020, www.businessinsider.com.

10. Bilge Erten and José Antonio Ocampo, "The Future of Commodity Prices and the Pandemic-Driven Global Recession: Evidence from 150 Years of Data," *World Development* 137 (2021): 105164.

APPENDIX: THE KEY CONCEPTS OF ADAPTIVE LEADERSHIP

1. See, in particular, the publications of Ronald Heifetz and Marty Linsky.

2. Adaptive leadership is rooted in an ecological perspective and can be usefully combined with ideas from evolutionary economics. One potential theoretical development could be to explicitly link adaptive leadership ideas to the insights from Carlo Salvato and Roberto Vassolo, "The Sources of Dynamism in Dynamic Capabilities," *Strategic Management Journal* 39, no. 6 (2018): 1728–52.

3. Ronald Heifetz and colleagues borrow the concept of thriving from evolutionary biology, in which a successful adaptation has three characteristics: (1) it preserves the DNA essential for the species' continued survival; (2) it discards (reregulates or rearranges) the DNA that no longer serves the species' current needs; and (3) it creates DNA arrangements that give the species the ability to flourish in new ways and in more challenging environments. Successful adaptations enable a living system to take the best from its history into the future.

INDEX

Lightning Source UK Ltd.
Milton Keynes UK
UKHW042124040122
396615UK00005B/157/J